JEN

A MEMOIR

JENNETTE BISHOP

Edited by
MEREDITH RESCE
Edited by
ELISA CHENOWETH

Copyright © 2025 by Meredith Resce All rights reserved.

All rights reserved. No portion of this book may be used, reproduced or transmitted in any form or by any means digital, electronic, mechanical, photocopy, recording or otherwise without written permission of the publisher except in the case of brief quotations within critical articles and reviews.

 A catalogue record for this book is available from the National Library of Australia

PO Box 880 Unley SA 5061

ISBN: 978-0-6459094-4-9— eBook

ISBN: 978-0-6459094-3-2 — Paperback

Some names have been changed where permission for use could not be gained.

Cover Art by Annie Millard Designs

Elisa and Meredith would like to thank Kiara Thomas for her work advising structural changes. Also thanks to Micheal Resce who helped us sort out the map, and Annie Millard for her work in cover design.

SOME NAMES HAVE BEEN CHANGED IN THIS STORY, THOUGH THE CHARACTERS WERE REAL.

"There are so many things that one needs to write about when starting a project like this and as I write about the different subjects, I keep thinking that I should record this or that, but there is too much to be able to do it. Take note friends and fellow writers, if you want to record all your story then you must keep an excellent day to day diary."

Jennette (around 90,000 words in)

ELISA'S FOREWORD

Writing down a life story that spans eight decades is a significant undertaking. Even more so when you decide to start your memoir at the Ice Age.

"I can't help it," Granny told me. "I want to explain how we Bishops got to Melrose, so I have to explain why our ancestors moved to Australia from England, so I need to explain their lineage too, otherwise it won't make sense."

"But, the Ice Age?" I asked.

"Oh. Well, I just thought people would find that interesting."

It *was* interesting - but her insistence on starting so far back did make her memoir a tricky thing to edit. I was nearly 90,000 words in and she hadn't even gotten to her birth.

It was after I finished reading her section titled "Enter the Kings of England" that I suggested she just start her story in 1938 – the year she was born.

She agreed, and the memoir finally started to take shape.

Granny was very computer literate—"a cool Granny," she described herself. But in the last few years, working on her memoir became a struggle. Arthritis was making it harder to type, macular degeneration was making it difficult to see, and constant software updates were making her files impossible to find!

But I didn't mind being called on to help. It was a gift, one I didn't realise was so special until she had passed. We'd always been close, but the time we spent reading, laughing and sorting out her story, helped me see a whole new side to my grandmother; and also feel a connection to great-grandparents I never got the chance to meet.

None of us were expecting her to go so suddenly. There were still so many unedited pages, increasingly out of order as she'd been determined to get as much down as she could, even if it wasn't polished. It was hard, no longer being able to ask her questions or clarify certain things, though Mum has helped fill a lot of those gaps. Still, being able to spend time with her words has helped me feel close to her, even though she's gone.

Shortly before she passed, Granny told us she'd written a new ending. Looking back, Mum and I wonder if she realised she didn't have long left. I regret that she wasn't able to see her memoir finally finished, but whoever is reading—whether you knew my Granny, were related to her, or just share a passion for history and storytelling—I know she would be thrilled to know she is sharing her story with you.

MEREDITH'S FOREWORD

It was a number of years ago when Mum started to write her memoir. She'd been inspired after Grandma passed away and she realised there were so many stories that had died with her. It was too late to ask Grandma about details once she'd gone.

So Mum began to write. And write. And write.

"Look out," my daughter warned me. "She has a very long introduction about our ancestors. And I mean *very* long."

From Whence They Came, was her working title.

Mum had always been fascinated with researching family history, so this didn't surprise me. It did surprise me, however, that she had gone all the way back to the Ice Age.

I would visit the farm house and she'd be tapping away on the computer, and she'd say: "I'm just writing it as I remember it. Telling it like it was. You're going to have to fix it when I'm gone."

"Don't you worry about that," I'd say. "You just finish the story."

As time went on, her health continued to decline but she kept on writing.

"We're going to have to think of a name for your book," I said, one day, when we were talking about it.

"What do you mean? It's going to be called 'From Whence They Came'!"

There was no arguing about this, but I knew her original name was not going to fit this story. So, dear reader, to honour Mum's wishes, please note, the original title of this story was: *From Whence They Came.*

But it is a story about Mum. Her larger-than-life character. A personality that was such a contradiction. So painfully shy, yet gifted with leadership and creativity. As I read through the final document that came to me after she'd passed away, I realised I didn't know half of the adventures she'd had through her life.

I could hear her voice telling me the stories over the months that I took to edit. And when I came to the end, I cried.

I hope you enjoy listening to Mum (Jennette) tell her stories.

We have renamed the book *Jen*, the name used by her family and friends during her childhood and youth.

SOUTH AUSTRALIA

1. Nonning
2. Mitcham
3. Delamere
4. Myponga
5. Willunga
6. Meningie
7. Wilmington
8. Booleroo
9. Royal Adelaide Hospital
10. Melrose

The many places Jennette has lived

JENNETTE BISHOP
Family Tree

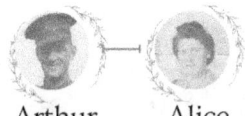

Arthur Hamlyn
1902-1966

Alice Hamlyn
1902-2005

Walter (Dick) Bishop
1898-1978

Ella Bishop
1900-1985

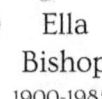

Veronica
1930-2008

Don
1929-1995

Margaret
1930-1989

Jim
1934-

Don
1937-

Yvonne
1936-

Jen (Jennette)
1938-2023

Stephanie | Meredith | Carolyn | Timothy | Lee-Ann | Andrew

Arthur Hamlyn was one of seven.
Alice Brown was one of eleven.
Jennette's aunts, uncles and cousins
were too many to list in this family tree.

1

MY FIRST HOME AT NONNING STATION

It was 1938. The depression seemed to be dragging on and on when Mum and Dad moved to Nonning Station in the South Australian outback.

Mum, Dad, Margaret and Don had packed all their makeshift furniture and had managed to sell their tent home. Margaret, eight, and Don, nine, were still young but they'd experienced a big move before, shifting from Adelaide to Iron Knob only two years prior.

Travelling out to Nonning Station on a truck, over unmade roads in the extreme heat of February, was no picnic, especially for Mum who was pregnant and very sick. The pregnancy had been a surprise for Mum. She'd been sick for a while, but when the doctor asked if she could be pregnant she answered with a resounding "no" as she knew that was impossible. Or so she thought.

Mum wasn't afraid of Nonning Station. She'd already experienced living in tents while they were in Iron Knob. and lived in many and varied situations in her life. Mum liked to tell everyone that she, just like our Lord and Saviour, was born in a stable, albeit a modern one. At the time of her birth, her father owned a livery in Adelaide, on the corner of Wyatt and Pirie Street. Mum had been raised a city girl with a comfortable life, but then the depression hit. She and Dad, like so many other young couples, had to find work in the outback.

After her time in Iron Knob, Mum thought Nonning Station would be easier. It was depressing to arrive and find their new home to be a dismal house, with walls painted dark green and only one room with board floors. The other rooms were dirt floors except the bedroom, which was cement. The home was isolated, apart from an Aboriginal camp just a little way from it. The other house was half a mile away. To make matters harder, as soon as Dad went up to the boss's house to report his arrival, he was told to pack a swag and tucker box—they were going out on the run for a week. Mum didn't even know what a swag or tucker box was, and was certainly in no condition to be left alone for a week with all the unpacking to do, and amongst strangers. But it had to be done, and Dad, once he got the idea of a swag and tucker box, was gone the next morning.

Mum had to go and make herself known to Mrs Hanley, the lady who ran the boarding house. Mrs Hanley took in any single men and was a nice, helpful person. She told Mum that she would have to make her own bread and was most helpful getting her started, showing her how to make the yeast out of potato. Mrs. Hanley also helped Mum organise schooling for Don and Margaret, and showed her how to send off for correspondence lessons. How Mum managed that first week until Dad came home was anyone's guess, but she learned in a hurry how to live on a station. Dad returned at the end of the week and finally, the unpacking and arranging everything to make the place liveable was done. Having a handyman for a husband was half the battle won.

Before long Mum was giving the children correspondence lessons and making bread as a matter of course. The house was made comfortable and they settled down to their new way of life. Margaret and Don soon got to know the other children on the station: four McTaggarts (two boys and two girls) and Mrs. Hanley's son. They learned to ride ponies and played with the Aboriginal children as well as the white children. Once, Mum was watching from her bedroom window as the children were practising their new riding skills, when Margaret fell off the horse. But instead of helping Margaret and bringing her to her mother, those who were teaching her to ride made her get up and get back on. Mum was furious, but she soon learned that it was the way of it in the country, and the right thing to do.

Mum and Dad became friendly with the house man and cook, Mr and Mrs Venn, and they spent evenings playing cards with them. They played poker but used chocolate frogs instead of money to place bets. The man who ran the Station Store couldn't work out why they needed so many chocolate frogs all the time.

The days were filled with work. The Venns had two little boys, who usually went to school at Christian Brothers College in Adelaide. Mr and Mrs Venn both worked in order to raise enough money to educate their sons in the city. However that year there was an epidemic, so the Venns asked if Mum would take their younger son for correspondence lessons. He was in grade two, so now she had three children to supervise, each in a different class. She also had to be ready to relieve Mrs Hanley of doing the meals when the mail man came. He generally had passengers that Mrs Hanley had to attend to. It wasn't long before Mum was making yeast buns as well as bread, and organising the schooling and cooking, but she managed well enough.

They didn't have electricity at Nonning Station. The only way of keeping things cool was a Coolgardie safe which Dad's cousin had made. This was a metal box which had flywire sides and a deep tray on the top and the bottom. The tray on the top had little taps in it and bags were hung around the flywire. Water from the top tray dripped from the little taps, keeping the bags wet. Excess water ran into the bottom tray to be emptied back into the top from time to time. If the safe was stood in a draft between two doorways, the air flowing through the wet bags would keep things inside cool.

The home had a black woodstove and a galvanised iron bath, but no bath heater. Water was heated in the copper and carried into the unlined bathroom.

Mum and Dad had a few visitors from the city while they were there, but of course the first few months were the hardest, as Mum adjusted to her new life.

But no one was allowed to travel on the bus after they were seven months pregnant, so at the end of June, when I was still two or so months away, Mum took Don and Margaret to Adelaide to await the arrival of the new baby. While waiting, Mum and the children stayed at the CWA Grange cottages. Usually, these cottages were holiday lets strictly for short stays, but because Mum was from the outback she was given special permission to have a cottage for the month of July. During their stay, Don and Margaret went to the Grange school, so Mum had a rest from correspondence lessons. After the month was up, Dad's sister, Auntie Olive, took Margaret while Mum and Don stayed with her mother, Grandma Brown, at Highgate. Here, she waited the rest of the pregnancy.

The night that Mum had to go to hospital, she had to walk. Though her mother went with her, Grandma Brown refused to wake Mum's brother who had a car. He could easily have run Mum to the hospital, but Grandma insisted that Lionel was a working man and he needed his sleep. No wonder Mum thought it was awful. They had to walk to the hospital in the middle of the night, along the Kingswood Tram line, to the Malvern Private Hospital in Winchester Street. It might have been only a kilometre, but Mum was in labour at the time. Grandma Brown dropped Mum off, then walked back home alone.

At eight o'clock the next morning, 14th August 1938, Jennette Ann (that's me) arrived.

When the time came for the family to go back home to Nonning, Mum and the children, including the new baby, caught the train to Port Augusta where Dad met them. He had come into the town to pick up a station truck which was there for repairs, so before they could head home all together they had to spend the night at a boarding house. It was awful —Mum with a new baby, and then the long trip home in a truck.

Still, everyone made a great fuss of me. Apparently, I was very good and would go to anyone. They all adored me, not least my big brother and sister. They had some extremely hot weather that summer. On January 11th 1939 it was 122ºF in the shade (50º C) and Mum stood and fanned me all day. There was no electric fan to turn on.

WHEN I WAS eighteen months old it was announced that Australia was at war with Germany. Dad didn't do anything about it at first, until, soon after the war started, a letter arrived from his mother in Adelaide.

"I am surprised that you have not come down and enlisted yet," it said.

Grandma Hamlyn was probably surprised because Dad had been in the Citizen's Military Forces for many years before going to work in the country. Whether it was Grandma Hamlyn's words or not, soon after the letter arrived Dad went to Adelaide to enlist. Mum wasn't worried. Years before, Dad had suffered from pneumonia which left him with a shadow on his lung. She felt sure he wouldn't pass the physical. But his lungs weren't the problem - he was rejected initially because they said he was too old at the ripe old age of thirty-six. Not to be put off, Dad joined the permanent army, and while he was at Keswick Army Headquarters, there was a call for volunteers for the AIF. Dad immediately stepped forward and this time he was accepted. Because he was a trained soldier, he was automatically given the office of Corporal in the 2/7th Field Regiment AIF. Before long and because of his long experience in the militia, he was promoted to Battery Sergeant Major, and later to Regimental Sergeant Major (the office he held until discharged in 1945).

Disruption and trauma once again. Mum couldn't stay on her own at Nonning station with three children. Dad's cousin's widow, Jessie Hollow, with whom they were very friendly, offered accommodation for us in her home back in the city. Her son was going to the army training camp for three months. So again, Mum and Dad packed up to move. Dad bought our first motor car, a Pontiac, from his uncle. They made the arrangement that Dad would take the car immediately and Mum would pay it off with the money she received from Dad's pay. Dad managed to get leave from the army so he could come up to Nonning Station in the car to take the family back to Adelaide. Once again, Margaret stayed with Dad's sister, Auntie Olive, and the rest of the family stayed at Jessie's home. Jessie and her daughter both went to work so Mum did most of the housework and cooking.

But the arrangement couldn't last as Jessie's son returned from training. Luckily, Mum's friend, Pat, told them of a house available for rent near her place. The house belonged to a friend of Pat's and she recommended us to the owners at Neweys Road, Mitcham. We moved in and got settled before Dad left with his unit, the 2/7th Australian Field Regiment, for overseas service.

One of my very first memories was the day Dad left. He departed from Adelaide to go to the ship that would take the troops overseas. I clearly remember Mum had a pusher for me to ride in. It was black metal with a child's padded seat. She pushed me along with Don and Margaret walking beside, following a dirt track until it met the junction that led to Blythwood Road. I have no memory of that journey to the train station but I do remember clearly being on the platform, and suddenly there was a train coming at great speed right up to our platform and straight through without stopping. Suddenly a rolled-up newspaper came flying from one of the windows. That was how Mum knew that Dad had gone past, and I would not see my Daddy again for a year.

After all that time I might have forgotten him if it hadn't been for Mum holding me up to his photo every night and teaching me to sing "Kiss Me Goodnight, Sergeant Major" before I went to bed.

Sergeant Major Arthur Hamlyn (Dad)

2

GROWING UP IN WAR TIMES

Our house at Neweys Road was only a small, four-roomed bluestone building set on the side of a hill. The hill had been cut away so the roof of the house was level with the back garden. The front yard sloped sharply from the driveway to the road. Halfway down the hill was a pine hedge which ended in a rickety old gate and five-wire fence. It enclosed an open paddock where horses were kept.

There were five families along our road. Our next-door neighbour was Mr. Fuller, a man so wealthy he owned the quarry over the hill near our back garden, the dairy on the top of the hill, and several houses (including the one we rented). The house on the other side of his home was rented by the Jamiesons, a Scottish family who all spoke with a broad accent. I became very close with Mrs Jamieson. Her children were older, and when Mum was sick she would often step in and care for me.

Across the road from our place was a house owned by Mr and Mrs Elson who were new to city life, having come from the country. They'd owned a property there and had sold it just before the depression. Times for people on the land were hard and at last the government stepped in and forgave outstanding debts in order to keep the farmers going. Unfortunately for the Elsons, this meant they'd lost a lot of money, as they'd paid off a debt that was never going to be collected. It may have been one of the reasons Mr Elson drank so much.

Next to the Elson's was a long paddock belonging to the Richardson's, who were avid market gardeners. I rarely saw them as Mrs Richardson was very sick and rarely came out of the house, and I usually only saw Mr Richardson from a distance, crossing the road.

I didn't play much with Don and Margaret as they were busy with their education. They caught the electric tram every day, first to Unley Primary School, and then later Margaret went to Unley High and Don to Goodwood Technical. Most of the other children in the street were around the same age as Don and Margaret so that left me with only one person in the street to play with: the youngest Richardson boy, David. The fact he was a boy made no difference. We spent a lot of time playing in the Brown Hill creek, swinging on the willow trees as we played Tarzan games, or catching yabbies and tadpoles. We also got a lot of fun out of the Elson's chooks. The fowls were always running across Mrs Elson's backyard and down into the creek, and she'd often lose track of where the eggs had been laid. David and I were much better at finding them. We liked to wait until the eggs had gone bad, then take them to the dry creek bed, find a big stone we could use as a target, and see how many we could break.

As the war progressed, our games changed to include things we'd overheard from the adults. By the end of the war, David and I often imagined we were allied spies whose headquarters were the air-raid shelter and whose job it was to set atomic bombs. We didn't really understand about the bombs but it made a good plot for a game.

The war had a big influence on our way of life. Once rationing was brought in, many things became unobtainable. Our diet changed as people had to make do with what they had. Breakfast was often bread broken up in some hot milk with a little sugar. Butter was hard to get so we learned to have dripping (collected from the fat on the roasts) on our sandwiches. Bread fried in dripping was a delight.

Even the world around us changed. Opposite the front gate in the middle of the road, a round thing was suspended on wires. It did nothing and I never really knew what it was for. There it sat until after the war, when one day some men came with a ladder and did something to it, and hey presto. That night there was a light shining down. Showing any light in the street was forbidden during the war, and the globes had been removed from streetlights, so I'd just thought it was a useless round thing in the middle of the road. During the war, we all had to do our bit to keep us safe. To stop the light showing from our house, Mum had stuck paper on all the windows and then blackened it with Easy Work, which was used to stain cement steps and verandas. At night, search lights would sweep across the sky making sure there were no enemy aircraft flying by. Though South Australia was a long way from the action, precautions were still taken. Mr Richardson even had an air-raid shelter built in the backyard, which after the war became a good rubbish dump.

The Richardsons also had an old dolls house which intrigued me. It stood about a foot higher than me and had broken over the years of being left in the backyard. The little verandas were just sticks that had supported the original top floor, and the inside walls had been torn out, leaving just the frame. The chooks found it a good place to roost. David and I often used it in our war games. But when I played on my own, the games were very different. I had my few dolls and enjoyed playing 'mothers' with them, talking to them and imagining their answers as if they were real people.

I didn't have a lot of toys. I had a rag doll whose red velvet hat, dress and shoes made up part of her body with only the brim of the hat and the shirt separate. I had a red felt elephant. Mum had made both toys. I also had a small panda bear—Mum had seen an advertisement in a magazine from the UK, that if anyone saved up their lead toothpaste tubes and sent them in, they were given a free panda bear. Mum saved toothpaste tubes then sent them to a friend in England. Sometime later the bear was sent out for me. My cousin, Pam, had a beautiful big orange coloured teddy bear which sat in a child's wicker chair in her bedroom. She had named it Oscar. I always thought it was a special type of toy called an Oscar bear, just as my little one was a Panda bear.

I asked Father Christmas every year for a sleeping doll and pram. Sleeping dolls had eyelids that would close when you lay her on her back. I was desperate to have one. But there was no such thing in the shops. Mrs Jamieson, whom I loved dearly and called my second mother, gave me a lovely little baby doll which would wet after giving it a bottle. It had belonged to her daughter who had grown up. Mum made the doll a lovely dress of layered frills in pink organza and it was beautiful, but it wasn't a sleeping doll. Mum made another big doll out of material using the face from an old celluloid doll of Margaret's. The nose had been chewed off but she repaired it with Plaster of Paris and painted it to match the face. Then she made lovely clothes for it using blue satin and floral voile, and she managed to get a second-hand dolls pusher. I was delighted and loved my new Sally doll, but it wasn't a sleeping doll.

Still, I had other precious toys—a tricycle which I could ride around the yard and up the footpath to Mrs Jamieson, and a child's table and chairs which gave me hours of fun. I also had a wooden rocking horse, the kind that is a flat piece of wood cut in the shape of a horse with a real hair tail. One of the boys who lived across the creek convinced me that if the tail was cut it would grow again, so it was cut, never to be seen again.

Although the war years were lonely for Mum, she set about making a home and bringing up the children. All the neighbours were good to her and she involved herself in the activities of the servicemen's wives. She attended the Comforts Fund meetings, and her knitting needles were always busy making various garments for Dad. Parcels were sent to the servicemen containing all kinds of things from home. At Christmas, fruit cakes were wrapped in grease-proof paper, put into tins and carefully sewn into unbleached calico covers, then sent to the men. I was the only one not at school at this time and so I also attended the meetings and acquired several 'aunties'—wives of other servicemen.

One of these aunties, Alma White, visited often, or we went to her home. She lived for the day her husband, Alf, would return from the war and they could start a family, and she was sure it would be a little girl first. She had a whole wardrobe ready and waiting for her little girl. Auntie Alma's desire for a child was so great that while she waited, she replaced the wanted child with a dog, a black Labrador named Pluto. Auntie Alma taught Pluto many tricks and treated him just like a child. I was very fond of that dog and loved to have both Auntie Alma and Pluto come to visit. But when the war finished and Uncle Alf returned, the family was started and ended with just one child—a son.

My uncles and aunties from both sides of the family visited, with their families. There were good times of playing with the cousins and attending the various birthday parties, with the usual birthday cake and paper hats and simple presents. Mum was always able to create something magical for us, even with limited funds. One year for my birthday she knitted a lovely dress with Fair Isle pattern at the top and bottom.

The Comforts Fund held picnics which we always attended and on one occasion an old friend from Iron Knob days, offered Mum a holiday in the country in return for Mum doing some sewing for her. So Mum took me to Yankalilla for a holiday. The friend's husband was the headmaster at the Yankalilla Primary School and although I had not yet started school, I was invited to attend any special class that was held. One such class was a music lesson, and I went along with the other children where I learnt to sing "Waltzing Matilda" and had a banana for recess. Each night Mum would read to me as a special treat. She would read a chapter a night from a book called *Alice in Wonderland*, a story which appealed greatly to my imagination. While we were staying there, Mum's sisters, Birdie and Una, with Una's two daughters, Raelene and Pat, were having a holiday at Normanville, the next town to Yankalilla. There was a dress-up parade being held at the local hall so they got together and dressed us children up for the occasion. Raelene went as a Dutch girl. I had hair so long I could sit on it, so it lent nicely to a Hawaiian dancer complete with grass skirt and paper lei.

And so the years went by.

During the war, help was hard to get. Workers were

needed for everyday jobs in places like the colleges and boarding schools. We lived very close to Scotch College. Mum was approached to see if she could help out with the domestic work there. She decided she may as well give a hand, and so she worked there for a time. The old order of things was still in place, so the headmaster of a college was still considered a cut above the ordinary. Mum was given the job of dusting and sweeping and serving the lunch for the headmaster's wife. I was sent to stay with my Auntie Hilda, while Mum did these duties for a couple of hours in the morning.

I spent more and more time with Mrs Jamieson, visiting or staying at her home when Mum needed a childminder. She had a real knack of making everything right for a child. I spent hours playing games with her. One game I remember was 'Going Shopping'. She would get her basket and umbrella, take me by the hand and we would walk around the kitchen, pausing at various spots where we would purchase invisible fruit, vegetables, groceries and meat. We were served by imaginary assistants and were always given some imaginary fritz at the butchers. Then we would catch the imaginary tram back home, making sure to use the umbrella to keep the imaginary rain off as we walked home from the tram stop.

Mrs Jamie (as we called her) had wonderous things in her home. One was an ice chest. There was an ice man who called regularly to replenish the ice in the top which made the bottom of the chest very cold. It was a lovely treat to have a drink of cold milk from the ice chest, considering all we had was the Coolgardie safe. Then this wonderful thing happened. Mrs Jamie's daughter had grown up and gotten a permanent boyfriend who worked for a refrigerator firm. Through him the Jamiesons bought a refrigerator, and wonder of wonders, we were given their ice-chest. I thought we must be the swankiest people in the world to own an ice-chest, and Mrs Jamie must be so rich to own a refrigerator. I was delighted to find that she was able to make little ice-blocks for me—frozen blocks of milk flavoured with vanilla and sugar and coloured with cochineal. What luxury.

Mrs Jamie always told me that when I grew up and decided to get married, I must first bring my young man to meet her. Many years later, even though I rarely saw her by that time, I told my husband Jim about it and we decided to visit her. As soon as we knocked on the door we were immediately welcomed. We sat down in the familiar old kitchen and I asked her about the little Scottie dog she used to have, but he had passed on. Then I asked about the big parrot who used to call my name and play with me when I was a child. "You wouldn't believe it," Mrs Jamie said, "but after all those years that silly old Cocky, he went and laid an egg!" It must have been too much for Cocky and he (she) died.

From this delightful visit, Jim was able to see a glimpse into my childhood, and Mrs Jamie was able to see the woman I grew up to be.

We never saw Mrs Jamie again.

Jen with Alma White's Labrador, Pluto

3

DAD COMES HOME

Wednesday 13th May 1942 0600hrs
In Aussie patrolled waters, a Yankee warship just picked us up. Strong rumour we will berth in West tomorrow 1000hrs. Hope these right as I'm longing to be able to cable to you and let you know I'm coming.

Bit worried as I have to put the S.U.S. off here while we are in port and have to take them on again when we sail.

THURSDAY 14TH MAY 1942 0600hrs
Well we will sure sight Aussie today.

1100hrs There she is Rock Nest, it's no thrill to me as I've a lot to worry about. Thought I'd be thrilled stiff but won't be till I'm rid of the S.U.S

1830hrs just pulling into the wharf, Freemantle band playing, no leave till tomorrow only a few people on wharf.

FRIDAY 15TH MAY 0600hrs

Leave today at 0930hrs. Have to put the S.U.S off first, did not get off till 1200hrs. Went out to see my cousin Ethel Lushey, gave her a bit of a shock but she was very pleased to see me. Spent the afternoon and evening there, had a great meal, the first since Durban. Back on board ship at 2400hrs. Weather very warm.

SATURDAY 16*TH* MAY 1942 0600hrs
Looks like rain, no leave till 1300hrs. Went to Ethel's again then went to see Uncle Tom Kay, had tea and a marvellous hot bath and had to be on ship at 1130hrs and it rained like the devil, got ringing wet getting home, real tropical storm.

SUNDAY 17*TH* MAY 1942
No leave, looks like leaving today
1300hrs got all the S.U.S back and we are at 1430 off to the home port where I'm going to disembark.

MONDAY 18*TH* MAY 1942 0600HRS.
S.U.S. behaving OK. Sea very stormy, rain. Yours truly is up to going to bed for the day as I want to be 100% when the great day arrives. Had no lunch but went down to dinner tonight. Now I'm going to bed. Looks like being in Adelaide Wednesday afternoon or Thursday.

DAD'S DIARY ENDS THERE. There's no record of Dad's actual landing in Adelaide or his coming home.

He'd been told he was to be sent back to Australia in March 1942, when he was in the Sinai desert. He'd unexpectedly met his friend Ron, who gave him the news that Dad was to return to Australia to be an instructor.

Ron was heading home too. They made an agreement that when they returned to Australia, whichever one got home first would ring the wife of the other to let them know how they were. Dad having been sent home on the ship carrying a lot of prisoners—S.U.S. stands for Soldier Under Sentence—had left the Middle East long before Ron. So when Ron arrived home, he asked his wife if she'd heard from Art Hamlyn and when said she hadn't, he said, "Oh my God, he's gone. He's gone for sure."

Thankfully, that was not the case.

I know very little about Dad's actual return from the Middle East because, as is often the case, I didn't ask Mum about it until she was 102, and her mind was failing. She kept saying that because Dad was an officer he always kept all movements secret and so she had no knowledge of his return.

But one memory was clear in her mind. Mum was out in the front garden, like it was any normal day, when she looked up to see Dad walking up Neweys Road. Without another thought she ran as fast as she could to meet him and threw herself into his arms, with a mixture of laughter and tears. It almost reads like a fictional story, but it's the one thing that she remembered until the day she died.

On Dad's return from the Middle East he was stationed at Fort Largs Military Barracks. He was there for some time. Soon after his return, Mum became very ill and had to have a series of operations. It was fortunate he was stationed so close to home so he could care for Don and Margaret. But once again I was sent to stay with Auntie Hilda and Uncle Bert. As time passed, Mum grew stronger and was able to take up her responsibilities as wife and mother again. After some time Dad was transferred to the Atherton Tablelands in Queensland, where he was sent to train troops for jungle warfare before being sent to the northern islands. However, before the unit he trained was sent to Tarakan in the islands, Dad returned to Fort Largs for compassionate reasons.

It must have been a terrible business. The men sent to jungle warfare were so young and had no experience, yet were shipped off to fight in a brutal combat they were almost sure to lose. Dad must have known what they were in for, but his job was to give them at least some fighting chance.

At the time, I was too young to know any of this. Auntie Hilda and Uncle Bert, with whom I spent so much time, lived in the residence part of an unused shop on Welbourne Street Mitcham. They had one child, my cousin Marilyn, who was the same age as me. We were the best of friends. Marilyn attended St. Michaels Kindergarten Mitcham, and I started my school days by attending the same kindergarten with her. But I was not happy there. There was another girl attending, Josephine, who had hydrocephalus. Because of her distorted head, none of the other children would play with her. I always felt sorry for Josephine and spent my time talking and playing with her, but this meant that I too was cut out of the other groups.

But I always seemed to have someone to look out for me. On one occasion, Auntie Hilda took me out on the tram. I loved the trams, particularly because my Uncle Len drove them. Uncle Len had married Mum's sister, Auntie Bird, and he was a lovely, lovely man. On this occasion, I'd had a wonderful time on the town with Auntie Hilda and my special toy kangaroo. When we got home and I was getting ready for bed, I realised my toy was missing. Shortly after we heard a knock on the door. It was Uncle Len. He had stopped his tram right outside Auntie Hilda's place to return my kangaroo. That was the type of man Uncle Len was.

Soon I turned five and was able to go to school like my brother and sister. The school that was chosen was Mitcham Primary, which at the time was opposite the Mitcham Council Chambers. I started in Lower One and my teacher was Mrs Taylor. I quite liked school, and it was here I discovered that I had trouble telling my right from my left. Luckily, I had a mole in the middle of my right hand, so I would quickly glance at my hands to see which was which.

I progressed at school as an average plus student and made friends with three girls, Carolyn and Diana when they were in Grade One, and Betsy who came a little later. Diana lived just around the corner from the bottom of Mugs Hill Road, quite close to where I lived. It was quite a distance for me to travel to school alone, so the children who lived across the creek on Brown Hill Creek Road were asked to keep an eye on me. I usually walked with them from the tram to the school in the morning and then, from the tram to the little foot bridge that crossed the creek on our way home.

Even at the school there was a war effort going on. There were big hessian bins in the school yards where all paper was collected to help the war effort. I have no idea what the paper was for, but apparently it was useful. Everyone was conscious of the war no matter what was happening. Then came the great day when peace was declared. We children were kept home from school and Mum took me into Adelaide city to the celebrations in King William Street. Everyone was cheering, hugging and throwing streamers. Happiness was everywhere. The government struck a special medal to be given to all the school children. On the day the medal was given out at school, the war games continued. As I walked home with the children from across the creek, we made up stories of how we had won our medal.

"I got mine for shooting down twenty German planes," was one story.

"I captured a Japanese machine gun bunker," was another. They were just games to us. How lucky we were that we never had to experience the real thing.

Sometime after the war finished, Mum read in the paper that a shipment of sleeping dolls had arrived at one of the big stores—The Co-op. Once more I got kept home from school to go to the city and choose the doll I had desired for so long. It was a hard choice as there were two kinds—one dressed in blue with fair hair and blue eyes, and one dressed in pink with brown hair and brown eyes. The dolls themselves were a rag body; it was just the head and the bottom half of the arms made of Plaster of Paris, and the hair was just moulded, not the real thing as they have today. But it didn't matter to me. I chose the brown-haired doll and lovingly named her Suzette.

I wasn't the only one to get presents. My older brother Don had acquired a horse from the milkman who lived across the creek, a big grey named Silver. He'd gotten it from a dare. No one could ride the thing, and the milky said that if anyone could stay on for a given time they could have it for a pound. Don, of course, had learned to ride on Nonning Station, so he said he'd give it a go. He rode the horse for the given time although it was not easy. He thought he could break it, so paid the £1 and the horse became his. Silver had a nasty disposition and on one occasion, when Don had gone inside and left me to hold the horse, it lifted its head from grazing and bit me on the stomach. There was much yelling and screaming, particularly when Mum laid me on the couch and cleaned the wound with iodine. Don never could break the beast but one day Margaret asked if she could have a ride. To everyone's surprise Silver behaved like a pet lamb. He didn't seem to mind a woman rider, but he would not allow any man on his back.

When Dad received his deferred payment from the army, he decided to buy something for each of the family. Because Don had his horse, Dad bought him a saddle. Margaret got a lovely chestnut horse named Ginger (which I could ride on my own – I'd learned to ride by being led on the Jamieson's horse Midget). Mum got a traymobile which proved handy for many years, and I got my long wished-for dolls pram. Dad also approached the Richardson family to see if they would sell the old dolls house from their back yard. I received the doll's house for my birthday, beautifully repaired, done up with curtains and floor coverings. There was even some handmade furniture that had been put away for safe keeping. More furniture came as a Christmas present that year.

The Depression was gone, the war was finally over, and we were a whole family unit again.

Don, Margaret, Alice and Art, with Jen at the front

Jen with the recycled doll's house 1945

4

AFTER THE WAR

It was a different life after the war. Dad had procured his discharge and got a job as a maintenance man at Horne's Glove factory at Prospect. Margaret had also completed her schooling and was working at Wakefield Street Private Hospital as a receptionist.

Don had already left school before the war ended, just before he turned sixteen. After working on farms on the west coast, Don decided he would join the Navy. But like his father before him, Don found he was not the right age. That didn't stop him. After some action he was accepted, but found he had to serve for two and a half years, rather than the usual two-year period that was allowable towards the end of the war. That half a year extra was supposed to make up for his young age.

While Don was in the Navy, he was given some leave and had come home for a visit. We'd become quite modern while he was away, and now had a telephone installed.

"Oh good, you've got a phone," he said when he saw it.

"Yes, we do," Mum said. "Why don't you call Dad's cousin, Ken Hollow?"

We all loved to visit Ken and his wife Audrey. They had a strange phone habit, though. Whenever they knew it was one of us calling, they'd say, "I've just got out the shower and I'm standing here quite naked."

Knowing this, Don went to the phone prepared. He dialled, put the receiver to his ear and waited.

"Hello?"

"Now before we go any further, have you got your clothes on?" Don asked.

"What!"

"I said have you got your clothes on?"

"Who's speaking?"

"Father Christmas."

"Don't be silly, who are you?"

"I told you I'm Father Christmas."

Mum couldn't help herself – she was laughing in the background.

"Who's that laughing?"

"That's Mother Christmas."

"Come on, who are you?"

"It's Don."

"Don who?"

"Don Hamlyn!"

There was a pause. "I don't know anyone by that name."

And then Don realised. "I'm so sorry," he said. "I've called a wrong number. Goodbye."

DURING THOSE MONTHS when Dad was settling back home, I felt a bit strange. For all the years we'd lived at Neweys Road, there had been no man in the house. I knew who my Dad was—the man in the photo on the wall that Mum lifted me up to kiss each night—but now he was here. It felt like a stranger was living with us, and everyone knew him but me. Still, his presence was quite a good thing because he could do all kinds of things that Mum hadn't been able to do.

In our yard was the Pontiac Tourer, a 1929 model, the old type with the canvas hood. It stood on blocks, having no wheels. I'd never seen it in action and always considered it my personal cubby house. But as soon as the strange man moved in, the wheels were replaced, and suddenly there was a car that we could travel out in. The car had isinglass side windows which could be lifted out and stored behind the back seat. There was a running board on each side, and a carrier rack on the passenger side which we could lift up to rest on the running board. It was useful for carrying things that didn't quite fit in the car, though the door couldn't be opened when the carrier rack was up. This car also had a manual windscreen wiper. When it rained the driver would find the little handle above the steering wheel and move it from side to side to wipe the glass clear. Our landlord, Mr Fuller, had a very flash car because it had a mechanical windscreen wiper. He was clearly very rich.

Just before Christmas 1946, Mum received a letter from her old-time friend, Vi, who lived in Moss Vale, New South Wales. Vi had to go into hospital for a fairly serious operation over the Christmas period. Vi and her husband had four children, so she wrote to Mum to ask if she'd consider coming to Moss Vale to look after the family. Mum agreed to go and decided that she'd take me with her. While she had the opportunity, she decided to go via Melbourne and meet up with Don who was stationed at HMAS Cerebas. Mum could also visit some other childhood friends who she hadn't seen in years.

The whole trip was a success. We stopped in Melbourne on the way over, staying with the mother of one of Don's friends, Noel. His mother lived on the second floor of a baby clothing shop, which she ran. I really liked having to go up the shop stairs to get to the house part. Noel came to visit while we were there, and took us to the station to meet Don, who got leave for the day. When the crowd alighted from the train Mum thought she'd never find Don amongst the people, but she didn't need to worry—he was so tall he stood head and shoulders above the crowd, and his uniform was easy to pick out. While we were at the station we had our photo taken beside The Spirit of Progress, renowned at that time as the fastest train in Australia.

When we got to New South Wales, we moved in with Vi's family where we stayed over the Christmas period. I had a lovely time with the four children. When Father Christmas came that year he brought me a penguin about thirty centimetres tall made of velvet material, black and light green. Toys were so scarce in those years that I loved every single one I ever got, and would remember them all into my old age.

While we were there, Mum found one of her old friends, Elsie, who she'd lost touch with. She'd seen a death notice in the paper, of one of Elsie's family. From that she got the address of Elsie's sister. Mum contacted the sister and was told that no one had seen or heard of Elsie for many years as she had run away with a married man. But the sister gave Mum Elsie's address and it was not far from Moss Vale, so Mum wrote to her and was subsequently invited to have an over-night visit with her.

We had our one-night visit with Elsie and her man friend stayed away for the night to make room for us. Elsie was a dog lover and bred little Pekinese dogs. She had a litter of pups at the time, and I really loved them.

After our holiday at Moss Vale we went on to Blacktown to stay with Essie and Eddie and family. Essie was Mum's closest friend in their young days, and she saw to it that we had a wonderful holiday on their little farm, Silver Lea. Essie had three sons and two daughters. While we were at Silver Lea I was able to do some farm things that I had not tried before, like milking the cow and riding on a sledge pulled by a big draught horse. We also visited Taronga Park Zoo, travelled across the Sydney Harbour on the ferry, visited the Blue Mountains and managed a swim at Manley Beach. It was a holiday never to be forgotten.

Soon enough, it was time to return home. We went through Melbourne again, and were taken to Luna Park – I had never seen anything like it in my life. We stayed with Noel's mother again, and she gave me a rag doll dressed in a long black dress with big white spots, a red velvet sash, and a red velvet scarf tied around its head. Just another toy to love.

And then we were home again.

But the war had made Dad very unsettled. It was as if there was something stirring in him that insisted that no matter where he was, he wasn't in the right place. It wouldn't be long before we left our home on Neweys Road, to begin a period of time when the family moved from one town to the next, again and again and again, as Dad tried to find that one place he could finally settle.

Jen and Alice (Mum) - Trip to Melbourne and Sydney 1946

5

FARM LIFE AT DELAMERE

Our first move was in 1947, to Delamere on the Fleurieu Pennisular.

Dad had an old army friend, Jimmy Barr-Smith. They had served in the same unit. Jimmy was the brother of Mrs Edward Hayward, wife of Mr Edward Hayward, later to become *Sir* Edward Hayward, owner of Carrick Hill. After Jimmy told Dad about a management position available on Hayward's Delamere property, Silverton Park, Mum, Dad and I went to Carrick Hill to interview for the job. While I played on the terraced lawns with Tom, their Great Dane, the adults talked in the library and the deal was signed.

And so away we went to Delamere.

To pack up and move to another house was quite a job, but Mum was used to it. Even we children understood the things that needed to be done. The date was set for the move, but there was a problem with our animals. I had my two cats and while Silver, Don's horse, had long gone when Don left home, Margaret still had her horse, Ginger. The cats weren't too much trouble as Mum had moved cats before. She placed them in an appropriate box for transport, and released them into the laundry of our new house, where she smeared butter on their feet. Her theory was that when they licked their feet clean, they also cleaned the smell of the old home off and would settle down quickly in the new place. It was probably an old wives' tale and really, they settled because they were locked in the laundry and cuddled and talked to by the family. But old wives' tales tend to stick regardless. The horse, Ginger, posed a much bigger problem but Dad and Margaret came up with a solution. They organised for Margaret to ride Ginger to the new home, staying with people who Dad knew on the way. This was a bold plan for a teenager to ride her horse over ninety kilometres on her own. Thankfully, Ginger arrived quite safely with Margaret on his back.

When we arrived, we were greeted by a quarter-mile long driveway, lined with pine trees, leading to a house in a big overgrown garden hidden amongst the pines. The house was a prefab kind of material, most likely asbestos, except for one red-brick room which had been added onto the front. Under that room was an outdoor cellar. Refrigerators were not common in those days, so Dad thought the cellar would be a good place to keep the meat. There was already room called a meat house along the side—a closed-in room with wood on the bottom and fly-wire on the top, so the breeze could waft through and keep the hanging meat cool. But Dad thought the cellar would be better. Unfortunately, come spring he found water had come into the cellar during winter, and with the warmer humid weather the meat began to grow fur and go bad quickly. So the meat house came up to the surface once again.

Delamere was just close enough to the city for friends and relatives to come and visit. Margaret's long-time friend from Neweys Road, Carmel, had now married, and they chose to make the trip with some friends. The men liked shooting as a sport and so they brought their rifles. Near Silverton Park was an old deserted mine, the Taliska mine, and they found this area good for their sport.

One of the first families that befriended us was the Hillam family from Second Valley. We didn't know at the time, but the Hillams were my future-husband's cousins, originally from Melrose, owning property that reached back into the hills of the Southern Flinders Ranges. But now they were southern state dwellers. They were a very musical family, and we connected on this front immediately. Music had always been a part our lives, as Mum was a trained singer; in fact, she and Dad both used to perform in concert parties, Mum as a singer and Dad putting on comedy plays. All through my early years, Mum encouraged us to sing together; and when the war came, she just added those war songs into her repertoire.

So when the family discovered Coral and Mrs Rene Hillam were wonderful pianists, the friendship only strengthened. Many a night was spent together, where they played all the old-time and war-time tunes for sing-song evenings. We didn't have a piano, so when another family, the Keys moved into the district and needed somewhere to store their piano, Mum and Dad were only too happy to oblige.

The Keys had bought a virgin block of land along a bush track, further down the Range Road. They'd built a galvanized iron shed to live in while they built their house. They were also dairy farmers and so in the best tradition of friendliness Mum and Dad invited them over for the evening. What they didn't realize was that the Keys thought that an evening out would finish at dawn. At 3.45am they were escorted out to their car and most likely got home just in time to milk the cows. On the second visit, Dad invited Ern and Peter, the farm hands, to come as well. They were primed to leave at midnight, commenting that it was time all good working men were in bed. But it didn't make any difference, the Keys stayed and stayed. Not to be beaten, Mum and Dad thought "third time lucky." This time the plan worked. It was a cold night and as usual there was a big fire in the grate and a heap of wood beside it for the evening. By 1.30am the heap of wood had disappeared and as Dad threw the last piece on the fire he said "That's my last piece of wood and I'm not going out for any more." In the light of the dying embers the visitors finally left.

MR. AND MRS. HAYWARD had a holiday cottage on the Delamere property. It was on the farthest side from our house, set at the bottom of a very steep hill, and could be approached in two ways: either by walking or riding the horse over the hills and straight through the paddocks to the cottage, or alternatively to go by vehicle (or horse) around the main road. The cottage was a two-storey place. On the ground floor was a big open lounge room the whole width of the cottage, except for a staircase at the end of the room. It had a big stone fireplace at one end, and behind the lounge room was a kitchen and pantry. Upstairs were three double bedrooms, one with an ensuite and the other two with a shared bathroom. Everything was exquisitely furnished. I had never seen such furniture and soft furnishings before. I loved to go to the cottage, although we only went there when the Haywards were coming to stay, as Mum, Margaret and Dad had to open up and air the place. We'd take the dust covers off everything and make sure the place was spic and span for the arrival of the Haywards. They always brought their servants with them, though the servants didn't stay in the cottage. There was a long building at the back as servants' quarters. A beautiful stream ran alongside the place and maidenhair fern and white lilies grew on its steep sides and right in the creek.

I did visit the Haywood's holiday cottage on my own, just once. I had ridden my horse right across the property and had been playing nearby the cottage. It was a way from our house and I was thirsty, so dressed in my outside riding clothes, and slightly bedraggled, I fronted up and knocked on the front door. Mrs Haywood, who was a fancy upper-class lady, opened the door.

I didn't think anything of it—I was thirsty, so I asked, "May I have a glass of water?" She was very kind and invited me in to sit down for a few minutes. I had no idea that there was a back entrance for the lower classes to use, or that it was bold to ask for a drink. My mother would have been horrified.

On one occasion the florist from John Martins Store in Adelaide, which was owned by Mr Hayward, ordered hundreds of white lilies for a function that was being held at the city store. Apparently they were expertly coloured and made a beautiful show. Folks may not have realised that it was our family who picked the lilies from their creek, which were then put into containers and baths in the servants' quarters until they were picked up and taken to Adelaide. But even though it was a lot of work, I loved it.

OUR DELAMERE HOUSE was magic for a child. On the side of our home where my bedroom was, grew a thick banana passionfruit vine. The vine covered the door that led outside from a small porch between my room and Don's room. No one could open the door to get out, except me because I was smaller than the others and could just squeeze through, picking passionfruit on the way. There was the makings of a dirt tennis court at the front of the house, and as Don and Margaret were tennis players, this was tidied up and used quite a bit. The property boasted several horses and quite a few wild and milking cattle, a Border Lester sheep stud, and a dairy. Margaret worked on the place as the dairy maid and general help for Dad. Don was still in the Navy so only came home occasionally until his discharge, when he worked with Dad for a short time. As for me, I had to go to school. The town was four and a half miles away and there was no transport to get me there. However, at the beginning of the new year, 1948, I was able to get there by riding my pony, Dolly. I was to be in Grade five. I rode through the virgin bushland on what was known as the bush track. On the way, I met one or two other children whose parents held land in the bush. Sometimes I'd ride around the main road and meet up with my friend Lillian who rode a bike. I longed to have a bike and Lillian longed for a pony, so we often swapped our mode of transport.

Mum always tried to plait my hair for school, but sometimes I wore it loose. Ever since my blonde curls were cut off at age five, my hair had grown and grown. I liked it long and liked bragging that I could sit on it, but it was also very thick and heavy, so when I was unwell Mum saw her opportunity and cut it.

This wasn't my only trial related to school. There was only one teacher, and he was an alcoholic. He took an instant dislike to me. It seemed I could never do anything right, and the teacher would punish me by not letting me out to play during recess or lunch time. I never knew what I'd done wrong or how to avoid this punishment. This created a chronic nervous upset in me which resulted in me spending a lot of time at home sick. After twelve months of this treatment, one of the other parents told Mum what was happening. I was immediately taken out of the school and continued my education by correspondence.

Apart from this, everyone settled well at Delamere. The old Pontiac car had been brought with us but only Dad could drive it. Margaret's horse, Ginger, was there and the family had acquired some dogs. These were supposed to be working dogs, but there was a question mark over that. After some time Margaret got a job as a governess at the Cape Jervis Station where the Bond family lived. Cape Jervis was not far away from Silverton Park and so I could ride my horse down to the Station to see Margaret from time to time. It wasn't far to go from the Station to Cape Jervis beach, and we'd ride down to the sea where we could let the horses have a swim. On one occasion when returning from a ride to the beach, I was on Ginger and trying to get him to come close to the big iron gate so that I could unlatch it without getting off. But he didn't want to do it. Eventually he got fed up being forced to do something he didn't want to do, so he took a standing jump over the gate. The trouble was he didn't make it and was left with his back legs hanging over the gate. Margaret hurried up to the sheds to get the men to help and they eventually had to slide him sideways to get him off. Ouch! I bet that hurt.

One of the entertainments we always attended was the local Yankalilla show. No one in the family had ever tried entering anything in a show before, but Margaret thought she would like to give it a go. The Bond family had a Shetland pony called Dinah, so Margaret asked if she could borrow it. She entered me in Best Girl Rider, and the pony in two Best Pony classes. Then she borrowed a coat and chose one of Mum's hats for me to wear. They bought long boots and gloves and they used my own jodhpurs and shirt. Margaret taught me all the things that I'd be expected to do. Then the big day came and off we went for our great experience. We won two seconds and a third prize, which was good for a first go.

Not long after we arrived at Delamere, there was a dance held at Second Valley and so everyone decided it would be a good chance to meet some of the local people. In those days the dances were a family affair. Everyone went, young and old. The older women took food for the supper and it was always a beautiful spread. There was usually a fireplace and those who didn't want to dance sat around the fire and chatted. I played with the children at one end of the hall while the younger generation danced. Don was with the family, home on leave from the Navy, and although he couldn't dance very well, several of the young women spent a lot of time making eyes at him. All had gone well for our first dance, but on the way home we discovered a heavy fog had fallen on the road. This was a worry as being new to the place, Mum and Dad were still not sure of the way. It got worse. Not long after we set out, the lights on the Pontiac failed. We were left with a very small torch to light our path, with someone leaning out the window on the passenger's side, shining the meagre light onto the side of the road. It was a long slow trip, but eventually we found our way home.

Another popular entertainment was a weekly picture show at Rapid Bay. The first time we went to the Rapid Bay pictures Mum and Dad discovered there were many old friends living there. It seems that BHP had had moved several families from Iron Knob to Rapid Bay, so there was an immediate circle of friends. It was a grand surprise to see everyone again, and the weekly picture show was a grand way for us all to connect.

It wasn't like theatres in the big city—the picture show was held in a long, galvanised-iron hut with a projector free standing in the back of the room. Hot drinks were set up on a table along one wall ready for half time. In the winter it was very cold and everyone came armed with their blankets to keep warm. The projector only ran one roll of film and so when that was completed everything was stopped, the lights went on and everyone waited until the film was rewound and the next one started. Dad always said it was not a good idea to arrive late, especially when a western movie was playing. He said when entering he felt he had to dodge the bullets, the screen was so close. It was all good fun, though sometimes the journey on the way to and from the show was like a movie in itself.

On one occasion, on our way to the show, we had another crisis with the old Pontiac, who by this time Dad had named Sarah. The car had just started down the Rapid Bay Hill, a very long and steep decline. Dad was a good driver so there were no worries about negotiating such a stretch. However halfway down there was a strong smell of burning rubber, and then to everyone's horror, Dad announced that the brakes had gone. Everyone hung on in terror as the car careened down the hill with Mum pushing her feet into the floorboards of the front for all she was worth, achieving nothing. But Dad brought Sarah safely to the bottom of the hill.

On another occasion, the family was going into the town to get supplies. It was a four-and-a-half-mile drive from Silverton Park. A couple of miles from the home there was a stretch of land that was open. Most of the land around where we lived was quite undeveloped and had thick scrub covering all the hills. However on this very open strip was the ruins of an old inn called The Pig and Whistle. There were many stories as to what was behind that name. One was that the men all went in and made pigs of themselves and came out whistling. The other was that the wind whistled down that gully, and the sound was quite loud. We were to experience just how strong the wind was when on this particular day, after old Sarah had entered the stretch, there was a huge gust of wind. Sarah's canvas hood had no side windows, just loose side curtains that fitted into the door. The wind rushed into the car and with no escape, whooshed upward and tore the roof right off. What a mess. How was it to be mended? In the end, Mum got out her trusty singer treadle sewing machine and stitched the hood back together again. The only problem with that was the machine never sewed quite the same after that.

Just about everyone had a run in with Sarah. Dad had a cousin who was an alcoholic and he was in a very bad way, so Dad talked him into coming down to the farm. Dad didn't drink so he knew if he could keep his cousin from going to town, he could dry him out. We had no spare room, but Ern, the farm hand, had a small house. Dad's cousin said he'd live over with Ern and Dad agreed. He worked around the place, doing various jobs. He used to take the milk up to the front gate about half a mile away, and always collected the mail from there on mail days. Dad was quite pleased that his cousin was keeping off the grog, but after a week or two he got a bad cold and asked Dad to get him a large bottle of Bonningtons Irish Moss cough mixture. This cold seemed to hang on and cousin kept asking for more Bonningtons. He was often sipping it in front of Dad. After a time he appeared much better and went back home. It was only after he'd gone that Dad found out his cousin had arranged with the postman to bring out a couple of flagons of plonk each trip, and he would tip out the Bonningtons cough mixture and fill the bottle with alcohol instead. We were actually watching him drink his plonk thinking it was cough mixture.

But when Dad's cousin left Delamere he nearly didn't make it, because Sarah seemed to have a mind of her own. On the day he was due to leave, Dad's cousin was already rushing to catch the bus back to Adelaide. With Dad driving, they'd made it to the infamous stretch of road by The Pig and Whistle going as fast as the car would carry them—probably about thirty miles an hour. Suddenly the engine stopped and the car did likewise. Dad was puzzled. Everyone got out to inspect the bonnet. Dad tried everything he knew, but he couldn't find anything wrong.

"Just turn the motor over!" Dad called to his cousin.

He did, and hey presto, she started. Off they went again, full speed ahead, only to have the same thing happen about 100 yards down the road. There just didn't seem to be any answer to the problem, but they kept going at a stop and start pace. Finally they made it to the town just as the bus was about to leave. Dad's cousin was loaded onto the bus and Dad was left to ponder on the issue as he attempted to get home again. It took a lot of puzzling as he drove along before he eventually realised what the culprit was—a loose ignition switch. The road was rough, corrugated caused by the big trucks that travelled the road every day picking up the milk from the dairy farmers. As Sarah moved over the rough road she rattled up and down. All it took was a certain amount of shaking for her to say, "enough of that!" and just switch off.

We nearly lost Sarah once, but one thing I've always admired about my family is the ability to rise to the challenge. Mum tried to be the hero on the day the cow shed nearly burnt down. It was Margaret's job as milk maid to milk about fifteen to twenty cows every night and morning. The milking shed was nothing special. One end was a milk room and area for washing up the milking machine, then the engine room, and opposite was a door that led into a big walk-in bin filled with chaff. The walls of the feed room were made of some kind of fibre material, with a lining of tar paper. From there on was the milking shed leading out to the cow yards. Alongside the shed with the chaff bins was a drain for when the dairy was washed out, so the water would run to the drain and out into the yard.

On this day, Margaret came down to start the milking but she could not get the engine to start. Everyone gathered round to see what the problem was. Dad was pulling things apart, trying to decide what was wrong, and in doing so had emptied all the petrol out in case it had water in it. The engine room was tiny with only a one globe light. Ern, the station hand, thought he needed some more light to see something in the engine, so he lit a match. Within seconds flames leaped up and poured down the floor towards the chaff house, following the line of the petrol. Sarah was parked on the other side of the wall with the chaff bins.

Mum let out a cry.

"The car, the car!" she yelled.

With that she dashed into the shed, up to the front of the car, and began pushing for all she was worth. Sarah just stood there in gear and with her brake on. But Mum knew nothing of such things, only that she had to save the car. Meanwhile, Margaret let the cows out for safety and Dad got the hose going and had washed the fire down the drain and out into the yard, which was a good foot deep in slushy mud. Sarah was saved.

She was given a break sometimes. Most of the family liked to attend the dances, not only in Second Valley but also in Delamere and Yankalilla. The only problem was that Dad did not dance. Sometimes he would come with the rest of the family and sit in front of the fire with the other non-dancers, but on occasion he preferred to stay home. As he was the only one who drove the car, it presented a problem. But the ladies were able to work out an alternative. Dear old Ginger, Margaret's horse, was tied between the shafts of a jinker that was on the farm. He was very good at pulling the jinker, so at last Mum, Margaret and me had our transport. When the Delamere dances came, we got dressed up, Margaret in her ball gown with a big coat, the rest in sensible warm clothes, and off we would go with our supper contribution in the carrier box at the back of the jinker.

It was while Margaret was working at Cape Jervis that she became ill. She was suffering violent headaches and seemed to be anaemic. The Doctor prescribed that she should eat raw liver to get her blood iron up. She did eat a lot of liver, but well-cooked by Mum. She suffered a lot of pain and eventually was taken to the Victor Harbor Hospital to have her appendix removed. Everyone hoped this would be the end of her trouble but in fact it was only a forerunner to something much worse. Though we wouldn't know what until a few years later.

Despite her health troubles, Margaret kept participating in the customs of all young ladies of eighteen. Balls would be arranged by different local organisations—the Country Women's Association, the Red Cross, or the School Welfare Club—and young ladies would make their debut. When a debut ball was arranged at Yankalilla, Margaret was asked to make her debut, and so much organising began. Dresses had to be bought, as all debs (short for debutantes) wore white ball gowns. Margaret's was made of spotted muslin. It had a square neckline with a large frill around it and short puffed sleeves. It was finished off with long white gloves. She also wore a short white fur cape for warmth.

I had to have a new dress as well. Mine was a knee length white crepe material with ties at the back, a peter pan collar and a huge amount of red smocking on the front. (I still have this dress in my camphorwood chest.)

Margaret's friend, Archie, agreed to be her partner and there were many nights of practise while they learned to walk downstairs from the stage, curtsy to the dignitary who was receiving the debs, and learned the chosen dance.

I enjoyed the experiences, but I wasn't ready to be a debutante yet—I was still enjoying my childhood.

JUST AT THE top of the hill before descending to the cottage, we had to pass through a neighbours' place. The neighbour's name was Peter Isaacs. He and his Swedish wife, Helga, lived in a small four-roomed house just off the track. They had a grown-up daughter Kitty, who'd left home to work in the city as a nurse. They had also lost a daughter years before. I loved to visit with Mrs Isaacs as I was very spoilt while there. Mrs Isaacs always allowed me to have anything I wanted to eat. I had a passion for boiled eggs and would eat up to six or seven for a meal. Mrs Isaacs also had some children's books that belonged to her daughter, all written in Swedish, and sometimes when I went to stay, I would sit up in bed with Mrs Isaacs and hear the stories as she translated them. Another attraction was an old gramophone with a number of old 78rpm speed records. I would play these records over and over while Mrs Isaacs taught me to weave on the loom she had sitting in the tiny lounge room. I visited the Isaacs' quite often as I could ride my horse around to their place without an adult having to be with me. It was on one of those occasions that I lost my special pet, Lassie. Lassie was a dog of questionable parentage. She wasn't very big and had a black curly coat. She didn't measure up as a sheep dog so Dad gave her to me as a pet. I had saddled my horse, Dolly, and taking Lassie with me, I rode around the road to visit Mrs Isaacs. I left it a bit late leaving for home and so had to ride my horse at speed to get home before dark. Poor little Lassie was rather overweight and she couldn't keep up. I got off the horse and tried to lift the little dog onto the saddle hoping to carry her the rest of the way, but she was frightened of the horse and I could not keep her there while I remounted. It was getting very late and had begun to rain, so finally I just had to leave her on the side of the road and ride on home. I was very upset when I got in and told the family, who by now were all inside ready for tea. Don promised to go and search for the dog and so he left in the jeep and went out to look for her, but he couldn't find her in the dark. The adults all assured me she would return by morning, but come daylight there was still no sign of Lassie. Once more the men set out in the jeep to see if they could find her. They did find her just where I had left her, but further off the road under a bush. She was dead. The tough run had been too much for the little dog.

There were other dogs on the property. Margaret had a part border collie part silent heeler she'd got as a puppy. She named him Shep, and he grew to be a wonderful sheep dog. Shep was the dog that went with us as we moved around the countryside. These animals were my main play companions. Sometimes I would stick a feather in my hair to be like the Indians from my books, with Shep and Judy, another of the dogs, in tow. Other times I would dress one of the dogs in baby clothes and put it in the dolls pram to be my baby, or else we would play hide and seek as we walked across the high clover filled paddock. I would lay down in the clover and wait until the dogs came looking for me. Shep was particularly good at this game. He always knew what he had to do. The horses were also good companions. Often I would ride off into the hills to play Cowboys and Indians all on my own. Margaret sometimes joined me in some of these games just for fun, but being so much older she didn't really want to play, especially because there was so much farm work to do.

Margaret spent a lot of time helping Dad, milking the cows every night and morning and then transporting the milk in the big ten-gallon cans up to the front gate. The cans would be left on the milk stand, which was built to be level with the back of the truck that would later pick the milk up. Our milk was then taken to the Myponga dairy, where it was used mostly for cheese. Transporting the milk was Margaret's job, and she did it in a dray pulled by one of the draught horses called Betty. Betty was a quiet old thing, and the dray was very handy for carting hay (another of Margaret's jobs) as well as doing the milk run. During hay season Dad would cut the clover with the tractor and mower, then when it was dry enough, Margaret would hitch Betty up to the horse rake and rake the hay into long rows. After that, Dad would pick it up with a fork on the front of the tractor and put it into heaps around the paddock. Then the baler was pulled up alongside the heaped-up hay, and the men threw the hay with a pitchfork into the hopper while a big mechanical arm went up and down and pressed it in, forcing it along the square outlet which held several bales at the time. When enough hay for one bale had been put in, one of the men dropped a square board in to separate it from the next bale. This board had grooves across it and Mum and Margaret or sometimes me, stood each side of the baler. As the board went past us, we threaded wire through the grooves and back again, tying it on the side and thus completing the bale. After that it was stacked beside the baler and then later, Betty and the dray would cart it to the shed where it was stored.

So life went on in this way. The Border Lester sheep had to be carefully recorded and at lambing time they were brought into the yards where the lambs were separated from the ewes, then one at a time the lambs were put back. When they mothered up, the ewe was caught and her identifying ear tag was read so that the lamb could also be tagged in the same way, and everything recorded. On one occasion though, Dad was devastated when he went out to work and found the very valuable stud Border Lester Ram he had bought for 100 pounds, had given up the ghost. Dad didn't know how he was going to break the news to Mr Hayward. It was never revealed what the boss said.

But Mr Hayward had plenty of other animals. Some were very strong characters. There were wild cattle at the back of the property, and they were not often handled. The property boasted a Jersey bull by the name of Tumby who was used to service the milking cows. He was a wild brute. He had no horns, as they'd been burnt off when he was a calf, but this meant he could not have a baffle put on him A baffle was a device to stop the bull seeing in front of him and thus preventing him from charging anything. The answer to this was that he had a ring put in his nose with a chain attached to it, and that stopped him moving in a hurry. However, one day Tumby trod on the chain and pulled the ring out of his nose, so that meant there was no way to control him. He was out with the wild cattle and not only became wild himself, but became the leader of the herd. On one occasion when the cattle had been brought in, one of the wild cows charged Ern who was riding his horse. The cow hit the horse right at

Ern's leg, with one horn going each side and knocking the horse sideways. Luckily they were near the fence so Ern was able to escape.

On another occasion Dad had taken Mum in the jeep out the back to see the cattle. Fortunately they left the gates open on the way. When they got there Tumby saw them and immediately charged. Dad drove expertly, dodging the bull all the time, and at last was able to head for home. He managed to go fast enough to get well ahead of the herd of cattle that were following, and he was able to get out and shut the gate. This incident sealed Tumby's fate, and the butcher was called to come and shoot the bull and take the carcase away. Poor Tumby.

Dad had a similar problem with some of the horses. There were two draught horses, Betty and Charlie. Betty was gentle and good to use but Charlie refused to be caught and put to work. If he was put in a yard he reared and bucked around until he could get out, even taking a standing jump at a very high cattle yard fence, breaking it down as he galloped away. Poor Charlie met the same fate as Tumby.

Farm life had its mixes of challenges and adventures, but overall, life was good and filled with excitement and friends.

But once again, Dad became unsettled. It wasn't long before the family learned that our life on the farm was over.

Jen's first ride in the Yankalilla show 1948

6

MOVING AROUND THE STATE

BACK TO ADELAIDE

We'd been three years at Delamere when Dad decided to go back to the city. On making enquiries he discovered that the house we'd lived in during the war was about to become vacant. Dad's nephew, Ross, had been living there, and he was moving to the country to take up a farm machinery business. Dad arranged to rent the same little house we had left three years before. This took the pressure off Mum slightly, as at least she knew where she was going and how everything would fit into the house. So the whole job of packing and moving began.

Once we got there, it was easy to place me back in the Mitcham School, and I was able to pick up with my friends from before. I also made a new friend, Betsy, who was to remain a friend through my lifetime. Fitting back into school life was easier this time. While I'd been doing my lessons by correspondence at Delamere, I'd got on very well. Now that I was in Grade six at Mitcham, I found the work was easy—in fact I was way ahead of the class. Apparently, that was often the case with children who did correspondence school. However, there were new subjects to study, which I enjoyed. One of these was domestic arts. This was an interesting subject and I learnt a lot of things that have stood me in good stead, because it was basically housekeeping, cooking and cleaning of the home. In those days every home had a copper to boil all their white clothes to get them very clean. But copper gets tarnished, and the interiors of the coppers would get grimy, so one lesson we were taught how to clean a copper with salt and lemon. After the teacher gave instructions, we had to get into pairs and clean a copper ourselves. As we went to do it the teacher called to us, "remember to use plenty of elbow grease."

I'd never heard of that before. I looked, but I couldn't find anything labelled with that name.

"Where do they keep the elbow grease?" I asked my partner.

She laughed and explained that there was no such thing; it was an expression that meant to scrub with a lot of effort.

Margaret was able to find work in the city and she began working in Rigby's Book Shop in Gawler Place. It was there that she became friendly with Anne, a long time and loyal friend who I'm still in contact with today. Rigby's shop was entered from the street and then straight up a steep stairway to the first floor. Just like her mother before her (before she became a stockman's wife), Margaret was not only a shop assistant but was also doing things like cataloguing and buying stock. Anne was working in one of the offices on the same floor in a different job; however, they became friends and soon found themselves spending lots of time together.

But the sickness that Margaret had before leaving Delamere continued. The shocking headaches kept coming and after moving back to the city she struggled to keep going with the pain of them. Eventually Mum took her to see Doctor Laurie, who had been the family doctor for some time. Doctor Laurie thought it looked like some kind of pressure in her head was causing the trouble, and so she was sent to a specialist who diagnosed a tumour on the brain. This was shocking news for the family and Margaret was quickly admitted to hospital where the tumour was removed. During the operation she came very close to death, and the doctors said they thought they'd lost her. Later Margaret told us that she was very aware of a tunnel with a bright light at the end that she badly wanted to go to, but something was telling her to go back.

When Mum and Dad went to see her after the operation, they were told that the surgeon had removed a tumour the size of a walnut, and it was amazing that she had survived. The surgeon also praised Doctor Laurie who'd picked it up in the first place, as most would not have. Then they were taken to see her. Poor Mum was horrified. There was her precious girl with her head all bandaged and tubes going everywhere, and the left side of her face had dropped down with her eye moving uncontrollably. But even in such a horrible situation Margaret was stoic. Her friends Anne and Freda were allowed to see her, and they too were shocked when they saw her laying in bed with the white cap on her head and her eye quite uncontrolled. Her speech was slurred as so much of her face was paralysed, but her greeting to her two friends was to gesture to the surgical cap on her head and say, "How do you like my Paris model?"

Margaret was in hospital for some time. Eventually she was allowed to come out for a short period during which she turned twenty-one. She was still a very sick girl and had to return to hospital for a further operation. The surgeons took a nerve out of her tongue, then grafted it onto the nerve in her head that had controlled her balance among other things. This nerve had been cut when the tumour was removed, causing the left side of her face to drop and the right side of her body to be uncontrolled. The graft would hopefully help the left side of her face and the right side of her body recover. While it never returned to normal, over the years there was improvement, but for the time being Margaret had to deal with the paralysed muscles. Later, because she could not feel anything in her left eye, the doctors felt it was better to have the eyelids stitched together so she would not get anything in it. They also had a large hook cemented to her teeth that protruded out of the corner of the left side of her mouth, to hold that side of her face up. This proved a big problem as, because the nerve had been taken out of her tongue, she couldn't feel the food on the left side of her mouth. Food would be pushed out of her mouth under the hook. She would be unaware that it was running down her chin, so Mum had to make some big bibs for her. If there were other people present at mealtime, I was always seated opposite her, and if she started to dribble, I would quickly touch the side of my mouth as a signal and Margaret was able to wipe her mouth clean.

Even with all these terrible things happening, Margaret never lost her sense of humour. She was always ready to laugh at herself. On one occasion she had walked down to the end of the road to meet me coming home from school. It had been a while since the operation and her balance was slowly coming back, so she suggested that I help her to have a ride on the bike to see how she went. Off we went, her riding and me holding the saddle of the bike while running beside. But it was slightly uphill and I soon ran out of puff. Margaret was riding along really well so I let go of the bike and slowed to a walk, but Margaret rode on, talking all the time. When I didn't answer, she turned to see where I was and off she went head first. But when I ran up to her, she was sitting on the ground roaring with laughter. That was the way she dealt with everything.

Eventually Margaret was able to go back to work; however, she couldn't stay at Rigbys. Climbing the steps up to Rigbys was almost impossible. So she found work at United Motors in the city. There she was able to work seated in an office where she didn't have to deal with the general public.

During this time, I completed primary school and started at Unley High. I enjoyed my time there learning subjects like French, shorthand and typing. There was also a music programme, which I loved. Dad managed to get a job with Cooper Engineering putting in lighting and shearing plants. He had a work ute which took him all over the northern parts of South Australia. Dad was usually away for a couple of weeks at a time but when he came home, he would take us out for various activities. Margaret and I, and Shep the dog, would jump in the back of his work ute, with Mum in front, and we would go off to the beach. We'd jump out with the dog and set off along the beach while Dad and Mum drove along the waterfront until they found a good place to sit and wait for us. When Dad saw us walking along in the ankle-deep water he would whistle to Shep, who immediately left us to return to his master. This was how we knew where to meet them.

Things were going well until Dad noticed that whenever we went out, people—many people—were staring at Margaret, obviously making comment about her face. Dad couldn't stand it, but he couldn't do anything to stop it. The crunch came one day when Margaret had met her friends,

Anne and Freda, to have lunch. The three of them were walking along, Anne having linked her arm into Margaret's just to steady her a little. As they passed two women walking towards them, the older lady said to her younger companion, "If I had to live with a face like that I'd stay home." Margaret, in her stoic manner, ignored it, but Anne blew her stack. She was so hurt on behalf of her friend. When Margaret got home, she shared this with Mum. When Dad heard about it, he made a decision immediately. They would pack up and go to the country where his precious girl would not have to suffer this indignity.

NEXT STOP: MENINGIE

In no time at all Dad found a job in the south-east of the state as stock manager of a station at Meningie. Once again, Mum was packing up and the family was heading south. When we arrived we found our house was a very small transportable place, seven rooms in total, but the rooms were tiny. Mine had a bed and dressing table on one wall, and that took the whole length of the room. The wardrobe was on the opposite wall and when I was in bed I could lean out, open the door of the wardrobe and pull clothes out. The other bedrooms were a little bigger, but not much.

I had to leave school at this point as there was no high school close by. We didn't have our own transport to get to a school further away, so I became a Jillaroo with Margaret. We helped Dad and Shep with the stock.

While we girls were working at Meningie we did a lot of work on horses. Margaret still had to be careful as her balance was not good, but she managed to ride on a little pony while I used the big horse called Fancy Pants. Eventually, Margaret became more confident and could ride Fancy

Pants herself. There was another rather nice chestnut called Enterprise who was a bit more skittish. He had the nasty habit of pig-routing. It was on one of those occasions that I was thrown off and injured my back. Although I always blamed that incident for my life-long back trouble, I later discovered that I had a displacement in my spine quite low down which moved easily and often became a problem when it pinched one of the nerves. Perhaps it wasn't fair of me to blame the horse.

We girls were always out riding and doing the stock work. We were also responsible for milking the cow every morning to supply milk for the whole station community. I also had to keep up a supply of rabbits for the dogs. This was a new skill that I had to learn. I was given a .22 rifle to shoot the rabbits, as well as learning how to trap them. Because of my rabbit shooting I became quite proficient with the rifle. This came in handy on all the properties that were home over the years. Much later in life, when a filmmaker made an Australian movie called *Twin Rivers* on our property, my shooting skills were necessary for a different purpose. The director was filming a scene where young men were shooting glass bottles from a fence. The only problem was, the actors were hopeless with a gun. If you watch that film, and see the glass exploding—that that was me!

But back to those years in Meningie. Another thing Margaret and I had to do was look out for certain weeds in the paddocks as the property was licenced for certified seed. On one occasion we'd been out to move some sheep. It should have been a quick job as we only had to put them in the next paddock; however, as we rode along, Margaret spied a couple of Salvation Jane plants, so she got off the horse to pull them up. I rode on but not far away there were more weeds, so I got off the horse as well. As soon as we pulled one weed, we spotted more, and soon we were busily weeding the paddock. Mum became worried that it was past lunch time, and there was no sign of us. Eventually she saw us slowly riding into the yard, both very weary.

The neighbours on the next station, the Smiths, had two daughters my age who also loved riding horses. Our families often visited each other. Margaret decided that she and I should try entering Enterprise in the local show. We were excited as we hadn't been able to do any show riding since we'd entered the Yankalilla Show during Delamere days. It took some time to prepare Enterprise and practice our rides, but we did quite well in the show and gained some prizes. The neighbour's girls were also there and they had a lovely dark-brown hack, about fourteen hands, named Laddie. Laddie's action was spectacular. Both Margaret and I fell in love with him, but we noticed something strange. The girls never took the reins over Laddie's head and we wondered why. We didn't know it at the time, but poor Laddie had been hit about the head by a previous owner, and now he wouldn't allow anyone to touch his head. To put a bridle on him they first had to take the bridle to pieces, then put a twitch on his nose so he couldn't move his head without pain, and then the bridle was put on, one piece at the time. Eventually they would put the reins over his head with a lead attached to the bit, so that the reins did not have to go over his head again. This took a lot of extra time as of course he didn't stand still while this was taking place.

One day the Smith family were invited to visit and they came in a jinker using Laddie. We were not aware of the complicated procedure needed to handle the horse, and when Mr Smith realised Dad had asked Margaret to go out and let the horse go, he was immediately alarmed. The men hurried outside to the yard to rescue the situation, only to see Margaret had already unsaddled the horse and was taking the bridle off—with no problem.

From that time Margaret and I decided we wanted to buy Laddie. We worked hard and saved all we could, and finally the day came when Mr Smith decided it would be best to sell him, as his girls couldn't handle him and never would. Margaret and I were delighted, and so we bought him. We gave him a new name used only at shows, Excelsior. We agreed we would never put a twitch on Laddie's nose again. It took us two hours to catch him the next day, but we did it and gradually he became used to having us catch him and put his bridle on and off without all the problems of the past.

As time went on we discovered that Laddie hated men, and we suspected that it had been a man who had knocked him about initially. He was so gentle that all the little children learned to ride on him and any woman was safe. But put a man on his back and Laddie would head for the lowest tree branch to wipe him off. And he had a mouth of iron, so there was no controlling him with the bit and bridle.

Life at Meningie was an experience, but it wasn't to last for long. The boss ruled that place with an iron rod. The other workers on the property were all migrants, Dutch and English. Only the manager was Australian. Whenever the boss visited from the city, he gave lists of what each person had to do until he came next time. Only Dad, who knew his work, didn't get a list. But the boss wasn't happy with the workers. He found that if he needed help with the stock in any way, the workers wouldn't do it if it wasn't on their list. This didn't work very well. The end came after nine months, when it came to shearing time. The boss hired a team of shearers, which in itself was no problem, but when he announced that he expected Dad to move Margaret out of her room and allow the shearers to use it and almost half of the house, it was enough. Within a week the family was packed up and sent back to Adelaide while Dad saw the shearing finished, and then he too left. The problem was that Dad made the decision to return to Adelaide, before we had a home to go to. Thankfully, various relatives took us in while Dad looked for another place.

INTRODUCING MYPONGA

Though we had to leave Meningie in such a hurry, Laddie still came with us. We girls were pleased to discover our new home would be a farm where Laddie was welcome. It didn't take long for Dad to get the job of Manager for Tolmers at Myponga, and once again Mum found herself setting up a new home—but this time, on a dairy farm.

The only experience Dad had of dairying was when we lived at Delamere, but his motto seemed to be "anyone can do anything if they try." Dad threw himself into the milking and all else. Margaret got a job picking peas for the Myponga market gardeners, and I also got work picking peas after school. It was back breaking work, but good pocket money. The more experienced pickers used to stack the peas so that they could fill the buckets quickly with less peas but the owners were awake to that trick and used to come around while the work was going on. They would just press down on the peas; that soon dislodged any that were stacked.

I was now able to go back to school and was enrolled at the Willunga High School. To get there each day was a saga. I rode my bike from the farm to the town of Myponga where I caught the primary school bus. This bus headed in the Willunga direction on a round trip to the Myponga school. At the point where the bus headed back to Myponga, all the high school children would get off at a T-junction. There was nothing at this spot except a tiny old shed made of pine off-cuts. The shed was supposed to act as a shelter, but, unfortunately, sometime previous, a child had thought it would be fun to do a dance on the roof. Needless to say, he fell through, leaving a gaping hole that allowed rain to come in. This meant that when it rained, everyone had to crowd into one end of the little hut and huddle together to keep dry.

The wait was nearly thirty minutes before the bus from Willunga would pick us up each day. If it was fine, we spent our time playing rounders or other games, or doing homework. But as the year went on and the season changed, it was freezing waiting at the corner, and even worse when it was raining. Now, I'd missed nine months of school, meaning I was a year older than the others, and so had a bit more authority. So when I suggested to the others that we should get up a petition to get the little shed fixed they all agreed. I went home and with Mum's help worked out the wording for the petition. After consulting the other children, I took it to the principal of the school. This man, Alec Smith, happened to be principal of the Melrose School in the days when my husband, Jim, was a pupil there, but at the time neither of us had any inkling about that future connection. Mr Smith read the petition and was obviously entertained by it, but he told me he would look into the matter. Even though the petition seemed to amuse the staff, it was taken to the parents' meeting. After a visit to the site by some of the fathers, the little shed was not only given a roof that didn't leak, but it was also extended and had seating attached to the walls so that we could sit down on those wet and wintery days.

Margaret, meanwhile, stayed at home and worked with Dad and also gave a hand with things around the house.

Mum soon had a garden planted and had all kinds of vegetables growing. It was here at Myponga she was introduced to sweet corn. One of the neighbours used to grow maize which was basically the same as sweet corn, and he had that for his cows. When the ears were ready to eat he offered some to Mum to try and everyone enjoyed it, so that became part of the family diet.

While we were living on this property, Dad had his 50th birthday, so Mum chose to have a party for him. This was quite a big thing as all the Adelaide relatives considered Myponga was a long way to go to a party. But they did come, and everyone enjoyed the day. Dad's siblings got together to buy him a present, and they felt pleased with themselves to present him with a card game called canasta. It consisted of two packs of cards in a box with the rules. It certainly wasn't much of a present from so many people, but over the years it has given all the family many hours of entertainment. It also helped when teaching the younger generation simple arithmetic.

While we were at Myponga, Dad decided to get rid of Sarah, the faithful old Pontiac, and bought a Studibaker Buckboard. It was really an old piece of junk with four wheels, but it moved, so it served the purpose. But we found we didn't go many places that needed a car. We were pleased when Dad managed to change the buckboard for a car, so when we moved again, it was in style. Sort of. It was an Essex —a very heavy car with gear change and heavy steering—but it was a car, and I learned to drive in it.

Dad gave me three lessons: one driving forwards, one driving backwards, and one driving in boggy conditions. During each lesson he reminded me to check the fuel, the oil, the water, and the tyres.

The first time I drove it on my own, I took the food for

smoko down to the shed where they were shearing. I was so proud of myself, and announced to Dad: "I've driven here all on my own, what do you think of that?"

"Did you check the petrol?" he said.

"No."

"Did you check the oil?"

"No."

"Did you check the water?"

"No."

"Did you check the tyres?"

"No," I answered, feeling quite foolish.

"Well," he said, "I don't think much of it."

ONE DAY, there was excitement in the house when a letter came to tell us that Don was coming home for a few days. He was now living on Wilkatana Station out of Port Augusta. I was particularly thrilled as I loved my brother dearly, and always rejoiced when he came home. But there was more. In his letter he wrote that he was bringing a lady friend with him. This set everyone in a state of excitement as we prepared to meet the friend he was bringing. When they arrived, everyone was delighted to find the young lady, Veronica Luke (Von), was a lovely, elegant woman who was very special. Margaret and I took to her immediately and spent a lot of time taking her all around the property and showing her life on our farm. We didn't know that this would lead to the disaster that threw terror into us all. Don, Dad and Mum had gone to the town to do some shopping, so we girls went riding to enjoy the fresh air. Margaret was on Laddie, I rode Sherry (a pony belonging to the Tolmers), and we had given Von the very safe and gentle Sandolphin, who was a retired steeplechaser. We were riding along quietly.

Von had never ridden before, but she was doing really well. But suddenly, Sandolphin decided to take off. He headed for the gate and, being a jumper, he went straight over the top. Unprepared, Von fell off, and the horse headed for home. Margaret and I came up full gallop to Von but the damage had been done. She lay on the ground bleeding, having fallen across the barbed wire fence and catching her leg behind the knee, ripping it right open to the bone. Margaret sent me off on my horse to town to raise the alarm. I've never ridden so hard as I did that day. I was horrified by what had happened, and what could happen to Von if we didn't get help quickly. The family rushed home and soon Don had her in the car and off to the Victor Harbor Hospital where she underwent emergency surgery on her leg.

The next time the family saw her she was all patched up, and Don had proposed, and she said yes. Thankfully, we hadn't scared her away.

And so Von became part of the family.

Marg and Jen 1953 (after Marg's surgery) Adelaide Show

7

THE LAST FEW MOVES

After a year or so Dad was unhappy in his job, so he started looking for another one. It wasn't long before he got another position in Myponga working for an Aberdeen Angus cattle stud. This was different again for Dad as now it was not only milking cows. The Angus cattle were beef/milking cattle, and they were show cattle on top of this. So he had to learn a lot more about cows. Fortunately, Shep proved that he wasn't just a good sheep dog, he was excellent with cattle as well. It was probably the Silent Heeler in him. But a new job meant we had to find a new home, so we packed up and moved once again.

The house that we moved to was quite small. Soon after settling, Margaret got a job as a governess on Lincoln Gap Station on the other side of Port Augusta, so the little four-roomed house was enough for the three of us left at home. There was no power at this house and so after all these years, Mum found herself back at the wood stove for cooking, needing lamps to light the way at night, and having to use a long drop toilet right down at the back of the yard. Dad still had the old Studebaker buckboard, so we could at least get into the town, which was not far from our new home. I didn't have so far to ride my bike to meet the bus for school, but I have vivid memories of the bitter cold in the winter when riding to the bus. I used to wear a pair of bunny wool gloves, warm and fluffy like an animal's fur, which would become stiff with frost when riding.

But the cold was worth enduring. I enjoyed my time at Willunga High School. It was there that I started my singing in public.

Actually, I tell a lie: I did have one earlier singing venture, when I was about four. The neighbour's sons had been home on leave from the Navy, and they were due to go back, so many people called in to say goodbye. Just as we were leaving, they put me up on the kitchen table and asked me to sing them a song. I sang my favourite:

BILL BUDGERIGAR DECIDED ONE DAY,
    To pack all his things and fly right away.
    He hadn't a coat and he hadn't a care,
    And he only had one green waist-coat to wear.

BUT THIS NEW singing opportunity was far more sophisticated. I was chosen to be involved in a school play, in the role of: *Voice on the Radio*. At some point in the play, the actors were listening to a radio—and that was my big moment. My radio role required me to sing a song. It was a small part, but from then on I was encouraged to sing, and it led to my getting voice training later on.

It was also while at Willunga School that I had the first sign of the dyslexia that would prove a problem for one of my own children in later years. I had been asked to read a passage out loud in the science class and after the lesson, the teacher, Mr Harrison, had me stay back. He pointed out to me that when I was reading I had been reversing some of the letters in the words. In those days they were not aware of dyslexia as a learning disorder and so, as it wasn't a bad problem, nothing was done about it. I only found out all the symptoms years later, when my son was found to have dyslexia.

I played several sports while I was at Willunga. I learned how to play softball which was a favourite of mine, and also played vigoro (a form of cricket), tennis and netball, known then as basketball. Sport was a community event, and you never knew who you'd play on the courts or fields. Sometimes I would have to play against the infant schoolteacher from the Willunga school; she was a very tall girl and a formidable opponent, but those few games were all I had to do with her, until years later, this same teacher and occasional netball player became the wife of my husband's cousin, Bob Bishop.

But time went on and still, Dad felt unsettled. Don and Von were married now, and Don was manager of the station at Wilkatana. Margaret continued to work on Lincoln Gap Station as governess to one of the Mould children. Then one evening when we had finished tea and I'd gone to bed, Mum and Dad were discussing the day, and a letter that had arrived in the mail. My bedroom was right next to the kitchen and with the door slightly open I could hear the conversation as they talked at the kitchen table. They were discussing an invitation to take a job as manager of a property at Wilmington, just about twenty-five miles south of Port Augusta.

I was devastated.

I would have to change schools again, and make new friends, leaving everything I knew behind. I began to cry.

Mum came into the room immediately. "Whatever's wrong with you?" she asked.

"I don't want to move again," I sobbed.

Being shy, I found it difficult when we had to move and I had to be the new student at the school I was sent to. The older I got, the more painfully shy I became, and found I could not look anyone in the eye if I didn't know them well. I would die a thousand deaths if anyone spoke to me. This discussion about moving yet again was just too much.

But it made no difference. Dad was interested in the job, which was to manage a sheep grazing property for Mr Maynard Mould of Port Augusta, who happened to be Margaret's employer. Apparently, when Mr Mould bought the property, he was looking around for someone to take on the management of it. While in the hotel in Port Augusta he asked the owner of the pub, "Do you happen to know anyone who would be a good manager?"

"You couldn't get better than the father of your governess, Art Hamlyn," was the response.

It turned out that the hotel owner had been away in the army with Dad. That coincidence led to the letter, and the discussion around the table.

Mum and Dad decided to take the job. The arrangements were made, and in September 1953, we were on the road again, this time to "Mi Kamp" outside of Wilmington.

Dad managed to make arrangements to sell the old Studebaker buckboard and purchase the Essex car, so when we left Myponga, it was in style. When we arrived at Wilmington we found we couldn't access our new home yet. The removalists had organised for the pantechnicon that was bringing in our furniture, to then load up the furniture from the outgoing family, so the house wasn't vacated for us yet and we had to wait.

We stayed the night at the Beautiful Valley Hotel and after having dinner, Dad stayed a while to chat to the locals and make himself known. It wasn't long before he found out that Mr Mould was not too popular.

"He's a hard taskmaster." The men nodded to each other over their drinks. "We give you three months."

Well they couldn't have been more wrong.

When Mr Mould arrived, he told Dad that he didn't believe in giving bonuses. The wages were thus and thus, and that was it. However, there was never a sheep sale (except in drought conditions) when he didn't say to Dad, "that pen of sheep over there is yours." At shearing time he would calculate the wool clip and then say to Dad, "that bale of wool is yours." So working in this way, Dad always gave his best for the boss, and the boss always paid him more.

Our new home in Wilmington seemed like a palace to me. It had a large kitchen and dining area the size of two of the other rooms, a lounge, four bedrooms and an upstairs attic office, two passages plus the bathroom and laundry. There was no running hot water so Dad got to work and made a hot-water service out of 44-gallon drums, bricks and lots of sand. This was heated by a wood fire under it.

The kitchen had a wood stove but it also had a kerosene refrigerator—what luxury. There was also a kitchen sink with water drainage; I'd never experienced that before. It had always been a big washing-up bowl and a tray on the kitchen cupboard. There was a lovely veranda all the way around the house which helped to keep the place cool in the summer. Things were certainly looking up.

When everything was finally unpacked and settled into the new home I decided to have a look around the immediate property, so I saddled up Laddie and went for a ride. I was disappointed there weren't any hills where I could gallop to the top and look down over the place. The only "hill" I could find looked like a place where a heap of soil had been dumped, and that wasn't even big enough to get the horse onto. Everything was so flat and covered with a small scrub-type bush. So different from the lush and hilly Fleurieu Peninsular. But from then on this would be the kind of country I would live in for the rest of my life, and soon I loved living on the flat, looking out over the Flinders Ranges.

We hadn't been at Wilmington very long when Don called to say that Von was to be taken to hospital as their first baby was due any moment. Don delivered Von to the hospital and, after waiting for baby, he came to pick me up. Together we headed back to Wilkatana where I stayed with him to keep house while Von was in hospital. Everyone was excited that baby Vicki Annette had arrived, and I stayed with Don until it was time for the baby to come home. While there I had the pleasure of riding some beautiful horses and as a payment for looking after him, Don said I could either have the money or he would give me a lovely little palomino horse that I had fallen in love with. I considered it carefully but then decided I would take the money, as I wanted to give Mum a gift from my first earnings. I bought a Royal Doulton vase which sits to this day on the mantlepiece in the lounge.

After Von arrived home with Vicki, Don brought me back to Wilmington and everything went back to normal. This time I didn't go to the local school as I was fifteen and old enough to leave. I needed to find a job. To start with I worked with Dad on Mi Kamp doing a lot of sheep work. As the work was always done with dogs and horses, it was an area I was well able to handle. Dad also arranged for me to go to work for Mrs Foster as house maid while they were shearing, and I started there during the week. Normally during shearing time, everything stops in order to prepare food and look after the shearers' needs, but Mrs Foster took the opportunity to get a few other things done. She was very difficult to work for. Every day while cleaning up after breakfast she would have me dusting and cleaning everything, including the jars of preserved fruit in the pantry. When the weekend came the shearing paused, and so I went home. But while I was out riding I had an accident with the horse, and fell off, spraining my wrist. I couldn't finish my job with Mrs Foster. Dad was furious. As far as he was concerned if you start a job then you finish it, but I was glad not to have to continue the employment. After that I got a job with another neighbour, Mrs Space. Mrs Space lived on Brindina which was next to one of the properties Dad managed, near the town of Amyton. She and her husband had a foster child, a baby boy, and she wanted someone to help around the house, including doing things with the baby. I loved working there. Once she took me and baby Jimmy for a holiday to Port Lincoln. While we were there the Queen visited Australia, and Port Lincoln was one of the places on her schedule. I was thrilled to be able to stand on the side of the street and see her close up as she went by.

Eventually I was offered something longer-term—a job at Edwards' bakery and deli in Wilmington. I was given a room to live in during my shifts, and I would go home on my time off. Most of my job was doing the housework, but during the lunch hour I had to serve in the shop. There were always a lot of school lunches to be provided, so they needed the extra hands on deck. I struggled with shyness and lack of confidence, but apart from this downside, I enjoyed working there. The staff at the shop consisted of Mr and Mrs

Edwards, their son Reg who was the baker, Reg's wife, a young apprentice baker named Pat Redding, and me.

They were a very homely little group of people and they were fun to work with. One of the boss's rules was strange. While we were on duty we could have anything we wanted to eat. This was a cunning move on the part of Mrs Edwards. She surmised that if her workers wanted something but couldn't have it, they would constantly be trying to get it. But because we were free to take a lolly or a bun whenever we wanted, it was rarely done. I satisfied myself with an occasional milkshake after work, but that was all.

Pat Redding was one of the local lads, a jolly fellow always coming up with ideas. When I first started work there, I found it hard to understand what Pat was saying as he spoke quickly and had a bad habit of swearing constantly. Reg gave me advice early on: "Just don't listen to the swear words and you'll be able to understand what he says." Despite his colourful language, Pat became a good friend to me and helped me be drawn into the teenage group in town.

When we first moved to Wilmington there was a regular picture show held each Saturday night, and our family always went along. But I struggled there, as all the young people would be waiting at the front of the hall and I had to go through them. I would settle myself between Dad and Mum and put my head down so that I didn't have to face anybody. It was a big help to me when I became friendly with Pat and his friends, and they turned out to be quite nice after all.

As I got to know some of the young ones my confidence grew and I was soon able to join with other activities in the town. I decided to go to church each week because the Methodist church was close to the bakery where I was living. I was the only young person who attended and all the older folks thought I was lovely. They did their best to include me in everything they could. Mum also attended church when she could, and she became involved with the various local clubs including the women's fellowship. But this wasn't without its issues. Once the fellowship was holding a trading table to raise money for one of their projects and Mum wanted to contribute. She bought a doll about thirty centimetres tall and knitted a whole layette for the baby doll. When she finished she innocently offered it to be raffled for the trading table. The women were horrified and refused to accept it. Raffling was gambling, and that was considered to be evil.

"No matter," said Mum. "I'll keep it for some child." And she did. It was given to her grand-daughter Stephanie when she was born some years later.

Besides the women's fellowship that Mum belonged to, there was the Country Women's Association. Mum had been a member of the CWA on and off, right from her early days at Iron Knob, so it wasn't long and she was holding office for the Wilmington branch. Mum encouraged me to attend the meetings, and she looked for opportunities to help me connect. Once, when the CWA was having some big function at the hall, I was asked to perform an item.

It was a big ask – but even though I was so shy in other areas of my life, I had no shyness at all about performing. But what song to choose? My music taste had progressed beyond *Bill Budgerigar;* I loved the hillbilly songs, as we called them in those days (they became more respected when renamed country and western). Before the Australian singers like Slim Dusty, American singers were popular. My favourites were Roy Rogers (and his horse Trigger), Hop Along Cassidy, and Tex Morton who often sang humorous songs, like "And the cat came back."

But we had just come into the musical comedy era, and I found a whole new love for those movies with their beautiful songs. So when it came to selecting my item, I chose "I Can't Say No" from Oklahoma.

This was quite bold. At this stage, I had learned all my songs without music, with Mum 'la la la'-ing the interludes for me. However, the lady from the next farm was a great pianist, and she said she would accompany me. I rode over to her place to have a practise with real music, and soon I was ready for my big performance. I arrived at the hall with just enough time to get inside and on stage, and I launched into the first line: *"It ain't so much a question of not knowin' what to do..."*

The song is supposed to have some humour, and I began with gusto. Mum had coached me to not look at the audience and instead look to the back of the hall. "That would cover everyone," she said. All was going well when I glanced down at the audience and saw a lot of frowning faces staring up at me.

What a grumpy lot they are. This thought caused me to forget what I was singing. I came to a sudden stop, looked out at everyone, and I said, "I've forgotten."

"Start at the beginning of the verse." Mum's voice floated down from the back of the room, where she was staffing the door entrance.

As directed, I started at the beginning of the verse, and while the pianist followed me perfectly, it was very embarrassing.

After this adventure I didn't try anything else for some time, apart from singing at the top of my voice while riding around the paddocks.

. . .

IT WASN'T ONLY Mum who got involved with the community. The whole family took part in whatever was going on in the town. One of the favourites was when the football season started. Mum and Dad had been avid football supporters all their lives, and it was no different at Wilmington. It wasn't long before Dad was part of the Wilmington football club's support team and he held the position as their trainer. This was a good one for him to have. He was diligent making sure all the boys were fit. He spent a lot of time giving them a rub down to loosen the tight muscles in their legs or attending to any weak spots that needed a bandage support. Mum's brother Arthur had been a well-trained St John's Ambulance man and he had given Dad the recipe for a secret concoction which he made up to relax those tight muscles. All the boys knew about this brew and reckoned it made a big difference when they needed a rub down, but Dad never passed the recipe on to anyone except me.

It was because of the football that I eventually met my future husband for the first time. During the time Dad had worked installing Lightburn lighting plants in the district in earlier years, he'd gotten to know his way around the back roads and where the short cuts were. On this Saturday the football was being played at Booleroo Centre, so we set out from Wilmington. As we neared Melrose, Dad said "There's a short cut through here somewhere and I reckon it's down this next road, I'll see if I can find it." He turned off and headed down the Orroroo Road. He had a very good sense of direction and almost immediately he realised he'd turned onto the wrong road. Seeing the farm gate at Gumville, he turned in to ask the way. Jim was at the sheds welding a piece of machinery when Dad drove up. Dad rolled down the window and after greeting Jim, he asked him if there was a short cut through to Booleroo Centre that by-passed the town of Melrose.

Jim considered for a moment. "The shortest way is the longest way, I think you'd better go around the road."

Dad didn't even try to decipher what that might mean.

"Thanks very much," he said, and wound up the car window. "What a bloody idiot he turned out to be," Dad said as he headed back to the main road.

Dad did not know this "bloody idiot" would turn out to be his son-in-law—but that is a story for later.

One day I received a phone call from one of the local girls who was nursing at the Booleroo Centre District Hospital. She had the message that the Secretary of the hospital was trying to find young women who might be interested in taking up nursing. I considered it. Up until that point I had always wanted to be a teacher, but there didn't seem to be any opportunities for teaching, so why not try nursing? I accepted the challenge and arrangements were made. When my brother Don was told of my decision he said, "She'll never be any good for that, I give her a month."

"Oh yes," I thought. "We'll see about that."

The first day of my new job came and I was driven over to the hospital by Dad, where I was introduced to the next part of my life.

8

NURSING DAYS

On the first day of my nursing career, I was fitted out in the nurse's uniform, but because I was only sixteen I was not allowed to have the official pink check that all the trainee nurses wore. Instead, Mum bought a nice green button-through dress with short sleeves for me to wear. It had a stiff collar and cuffs attached to the dress. Over the top I wore a stiff white apron which had two wide straps that crossed around me. The skirt of the apron went right around me, leaving an opening at the back.

In the city, training took three years to complete and started at the age of eighteen. In the country the girls could start at seventeen for a four-year training period. However, it was possible for girls to start their nursing training at an earlier age if it was agreeable to the hospital. Although I did exactly the same work as any other trainee, my actual training didn't start until I was seventeen. I started in January, but the training officially began on my seventeenth birthday in August. It took the four years plus an extra eight months to complete the course.

I was shown the nurses' home to start with, so I could put my belongings away and learn about the off-duty living arrangements. The nurses' home was a building with a passage down the centre. There were bedrooms each side of the passage, but these were the domain of the trained staff. On the left side was the toilet, bathroom and nurses' lounge room, and on the other side was the night staff sleeping room, and one long room called the dressing room. The passage opened out onto a closed-in veranda with a door at the end that led to the back of the hospital. This was where we trainees were to sleep.

The veranda was closed in with flywire and blinds, and the door separating us from the outside was kept closed with a spring clip. It was cold but we managed to keep dry, because right along the edge of the wall was a little gutter which prevented our bedroom from flooding when there were heavy rains. The water would come in between the flywire and run down the wall.

There were six old, black iron beds in our veranda-sleep-out, but the wire mattresses were so old they drooped right down, and when we got into bed we sank so low, an onlooker could hardly tell we were there. On one night, we had all gone to bed and I had settled down, laying on my stomach with my pillow over my head, as was my habit. It was a nice cosy position. Suddenly the outside door flung open, and Sister Selor hurried in. She got level with my bed and said, "Where is Hamlyn, why isn't she in bed?"

"I'm here." I said, pulling my head out from under my pillow.

Sister Selor was amazed. The dip in the bed meant the blankets were almost level, and it looked as if the bed was made.

The veranda was only for sleeping. When we were ready

to get up we went into the long dressing room which was set up just for us. In this room there were six dressing tables, back-to-back down the centre of the room, and opposite each was a wardrobe and a chair. There was also a set of lockers at the end of the room, one for each of us to keep any valuables. Each area was considered your 'corner,' and we were expected to keep it tidy and have our things put away. None of us were very good at keeping things tidy, including me. We always seemed to have a mess all over our dressing table and chair, and sometimes it seemed there was nowhere to put your feet. One day, after I had been nursing for several months, I came in and couldn't find what I wanted amongst the mess on my dressing table. I looked up at the end of the room where there was one dressing table that was always immaculate. It belonged to Margaret, and I thought, "If she can keep her corner tidy, why shouldn't I?" So, I tidied my area up and from then on, I never let it get in a mess again.

The do's and don'ts of the job were straightforward. I must make my bed in the nurse's home; there were to be no male visitors; I must be in bed by 9.30pm unless I had a pass (only one pass per week). Working shifts were either 6am to 3pm, or 6am to 11am a break and resume from 5pm to 8pm; or 11am to 8pm. Night shift was from 7pm to 7am and lasted for fourteen nights straight, with two days off afterwards. I was to always keep myself tidy and wear a good deodorant. At the beginning of each duty shift we had to go around and greet each patient. At the beginning of night duty, we had to remove all flowers from the bedrooms and place them on a table in the courtyard for the night. In the morning the registered nurse or senior nurse would give the flowers fresh water and dispose of any that were dead. My wage was £6 per fortnight, plus meals at the hospital and uniforms. This was a very low wage at the time, but it was the first one I had ever had, so I was satisfied.

DAY SHIFTS WERE ALWAYS BUSY. Beginning at 6am, we'd gather in the office and were given a report on everything that happened during the night. Each shift had two trainee nurses and one registered nurse, who was always addressed as Sister. After receiving the report, each nurse would go to their patients and begin the daily procedure. The sister or senior nurse would attend to medications, the others would go to patients with a bowl of hot water and towels and help give each one a good sponge bath. Almost no one was showered, they were all bed bathed. After that was put away and cleaned up, the patient was ready to receive their visit from the doctor. Breakfasts were served at the same time as the doctor was making his rounds, so we'd take these out to the patients on trays. The private rooms got a small pot of tea plus a jug of milk, while the public patients just got a cup of tea already poured. The same thing happened at morning-tea, afternoon-tea and supper—the private patients got the teapot and all the works on a special tray, while the public patients got what was given to them.

Once everyone was fed the staff had their meal. We ate together at the same time, and if there was a patient bell that needed answering, the junior nurse on duty was responsible for seeing to it. After breakfast we'd go to the table in the hospital courtyard and check the small book in which the doctor had written up the orders for each patient. Then we would get straight to it.

Booleroo Hospital was quite small, approximately thirty-two beds. The hospital consisted of one long building with a courtyard in the middle. The courtyard had a roof around it like a veranda, but the middle section was open. The centre of the floor sloped in slightly, as it covered an underground tank, and the water that came in from the rain just ran straight into the tank. Patients sometimes sat out in the courtyard so they could watch the world go by, but they weren't always warm and comfortable.

When I first started at the hospital, the staff consisted of Doctor Stevenson, Matron Denner, Sister Selor and Sister Betson, plus five nurses (including me), one housemaid, Mrs Mac the cook, and Charlie Brown the yard man. The hospital was run by a board of local people, administrated by the Secretary, Mr Bob.

Although there was a housemaid, she also filled in as kitchen maid, and so the nurses had to pick up a lot of the cleaning. It was our job to dust all the rooms as we went about our daily chores, and when a patient was discharged from the private rooms, we stripped everything. The furniture was washed down and the beds were taken outside in the sun to sterilise them. While patients were out of the room, the wooden floors had to be washed and polished, and this was done on our hands and knees. We would tuck our white aprons up around our waists so the polish wouldn't get on them, and then using a polish stain, we polished the floors by hand.

In the winter it was the job of the early morning nurses to make sure there was a fire burning in every room, so we had to clean out the fireplace from the previous night's ashes, set a new fire and get it burning, and bring in extra wood to keep it going during the day. Charlie Brown kept the wood chopped and stacked by the back door. It was often difficult to get the fire going in the morning as there was no such thing as firelighters, but each room had a hollow piece of tubing that served as a poker for the fire, and if we lit some paper under the wood and blew through the poker, it would act like a bellows and get the flames jumping very well. The junior nurse on duty had the unenviable job of cleaning all the pans and bottles that had been for toileting, ensuring they were ready for use that day. After that she was responsible for making sure any extra soiled linen had been washed before it was sent to the laundry. This meant that sheets that had been dirtied, any dirty nappies and anything soiled with blood were all put in the back veranda where there was a big cement wash trough, and the junior nurse had to wash them by hand in cold water before they were sent to the laundry in an old pram. It was hard work but because everyone had their turn at doing all these things, no one cared. We just got on with the job. Of course, we had our time off to relieve the strain of it all. Though I must say I was relieved when I was no longer the junior nurse.

All the staff had to live at the nurses' home, with all its rules and restrictions, so it was only when we had our days off and went to our real homes that we were free to do what we wanted. However, when there were girls on staff who lived in Booleroo, we were allowed to visit them in our hours off between shifts. One such girl was Pat, who started at the hospital well after me. We got on very well and she often invited me to her house for afternoon tea, which broke the monotony. Pat also came and stayed at our place a few times, when we were both off together.

On one occasion I'd just finished night duty and Dad allowed me to have the car so I could get home quickly for the weekend. Usually I'd go to bed at the hospital, then catch the Barwells Bull, a railcar that would take me from Booleroo to Wilmington. But the train didn't leave until

3.30pm on Saturday and by then, the weekend was nearly over. This time I felt quite in control of things, being allowed to drive the car home. I decided I wouldn't waste time—I'd get into my night clothes. Toasty warm in my dressing gown and slippers, I left for home. It was early in the morning, and I knew there wouldn't be anyone on the road at that hour. But when I came to the S bend the other side of Melrose, I was horrified to find a mob of sheep being pushed over the train line, and they did not want to be pushed. I had to stop and wait, and I was most embarrassed when the owner of the sheep came up to me and said, "Hello Nurse, you're out early."

Oh, the embarrassment—it was some of our neighbours, a father and sons, whom I knew well. Because I was in my night clothes, I didn't get out of the car and give a hand.

In those days no nurses were married. When any of the girls got married, they were required to resign, and only if their husband died were they allowed to continue working. There was one exception. A married nurse at the Royal Adelaide Hospital, whose husband was disabled, so she had special dispensation and was allowed to work. The rest of us were all single, so you can imagine we could be a handful.

Poor Matron Denner found I was a bit much for her at times. Although I was still very shy, I had been brought up to think for myself, and I was coming up with ideas all the time. At one part of the piece, I was on night duty, and things were very slow at the hospital. We had gotten on with our work quickly, and then found ourselves in those wee hours with little to do. It was hard to keep awake. During one of these night shifts I had been struggling to keep my eyes open and so I started considering what there was in the town of Booleroo Centre that would make me want to stay there.

The town didn't have a great reputation, often described as a place you went under duress because there was simply nothing there. My companion and I were discussing it, and she mentioned that you couldn't even get Coca Cola in the town. I didn't particularly like Coca Cola, but it was too good an opportunity to miss taking action, so I suggested we write to Coca Cola and tell them they should do something about it. I figured I knew how to go about it—I'd sent a petition into the school about the bus shelter which got good attention. We sat down and composed a lovely letter to Coca Cola and carefully addressed it. On my next day off I went to the post office and sent it, thinking that would be the last we heard of it. But no. Shortly after, two young men appeared at the door of the hospital and asked to see me and my partner in crime. Sheepishly we went to the door and were surprised to find a crate of Coca Cola, plus an invitation from the two young gentlemen to join them for dinner at the hotel. We thanked them for the Coke and accepted the dinner date, followed by a sound telling off from Matron Denner who declared she didn't know what to do with such reprobate girls.

Matron Denner was only at the hospital for about a year after I started, but she had some odd ideas about how things should be done. Brownie (the groundsman) was a very obliging little man and never missed a day's work. In fact, he never had a day off. After several years the board noticed that he'd had no holidays and decided he should be allowed to go away for two weeks. Everything was arranged, but the main reason Brownie had never taken time off was that he had to milk the cow for the hospital. That had always been the hiccup in his plans for a holiday—who would milk the cow? Everyone was talking about it and when I heard the problem, I said, "I can milk the cow." Mr Bob, who had been organising the whole thing, was delighted. It was agreed that I would get up at the usual time, do the milking, come in, wash and get togged up in my uniform, then go on duty for the rest of the shift. Then I would milk the cow again in the evening. This was all arranged while Matron was on her day off. When she came back on duty at 11am that day, imagine the ruckus when she found out I had milked the cow. She was furious and made it quite clear it had to stop.

"I can't have my nurses out amongst the animals and then coming in to attend to the patients!" she stormed.

Poor Mr Bob had to do some fast thinking to find a farmer who would willingly take the job on.

Despite Matron Denner's insistence that animals and nurses didn't go well together, she had a tiny dog, a Chihuahua. She carried it around everywhere she went, even when on duty. She even used to take it into the wards and put it into the bed with various patients. This caused a problem when they objected to having a dog put in their bed, but she was the Matron and no one argued with her. Eventually, some patient complained to the board and so it became the responsibility of Mr Bob to tell her she had to leave the dog out of the hospital. That did not go down well, but the solution came in a sad way in the end.

I was on night duty and I heard a lot of noise coming from the kitchen. The kitchen was closed and there shouldn't have been anyone in there. When I went to investigate the noise, I found Matron Denner and two other people with the dog on the table, and they were obviously forcing water down its throat. It appeared that Matron had guests in her flat for the evening and while they were sitting and enjoying each other's company, she suddenly saw the dog eating something off the floor. She realised it was her tablets that had fallen somehow, and she knew they were potent. She grabbed the dog and headed for the kitchen to get salt water into the creature to try make it vomit. But it was to no avail. The little dog died, and so did the problems in the hospital.

About three months into my training 1953

Jen, seated right, with other trainee nurses, Booleroo Centre

9

GAINING MORE EXPERIENCE

After a year of nursing, I was enjoying my work. My parents were getting good reports from people I'd cared for while in hospital, and I was feeling more confident. Then came the news that we were getting a new Matron. Matron Denner had resigned.

Everyone was looking forward to meeting their new boss and so they were surprised to find that it was Matron Lorna Catford, a woman originally from the area. She was much older than we teenage nurses, but was definitely one of us, having family close and knowing many people in the district. She also had a sense of humour, often bringing some joke or other to the table at breakfast. As soon as she took the position, she made several changes, bringing things up to more modern standards. When she met me for the first time she said, "Yes, you're the one who should have had holidays." I was pleased to hear this as I was a month overdue for leave, but that had never worried Matron Denner.

I was now seventeen and officially training, so I was signed up to study anatomy and physiology. This meant going to a weekly lecture delivered by Doctor Stevenson. Doctor Stevenson was a nice man and a good doctor, but he was very short, very quiet, and he often seemed nervous around the Matron. His lectures were not very informative—basically he would read us a chapter from the textbook until the whole textbook had been talked through. Other than that it was up to the nurses to learn everything that was in the book. How any of them passed, no one knows, but they mostly did.

Besides the study we did with the doctor, we learned many things from the senior staff. It's all very well to learn things from books, and know ideas and theories in your head, but there's nothing like putting them into practise. Somehow it all begins to make sense when you have to actually do it. Such was the case when I had to learn to give an injection. The sister on duty at the time, Sister Banks, lined me up to learn this skill. She selected one of the male patients who was willing to "give it a go" for me to inject. He was a gentleman who'd been visiting the district from the Riverland, and he'd had his appendix removed. It was usual for new nurses to practise injecting an orange or apple before attacking their first patient. I'd practiced on plenty of fruit, so I felt confident I could do the job. The injection was penicillin, and this required the patient to bare his bottom, which gave plenty of room to inject without missing. Sister Banks explained how to select the right area by dividing the buttocks into quarters and aiming for the top quarter. So after marking the spot, I took the syringe and plunged the needle into the selected point. Or so I thought. No one had told me how tough the human skin is—it didn't feel like an orange at all as the needle bounced back at me. I had to have another go, but I still couldn't get it to go into the poor man's flesh. After a third unsuccessful try, Sister Banks grabbed the syringe and cried, "Give it to me! I can't let you go on puncturing the poor patient that way!" So my first attempt at giving an injection was a failure, and I was sent back to practice with the fruit. This incident stayed in my mind for some time. When any new nurses came to this part of their training I always volunteered to allow them to give me fake injections in my arm, so they would know what it felt like before having to do the real thing.

As a side note—a couple of years later I met the man who was the recipient of my first unfortunate injection when he came to stay with his sister-in-law, Mrs Ella Bishop. Yes, it turned out to be Jim's uncle, Warren Ekins. What luck.

Six months after Matron Catford started, she announced there was going to be a surprise happening soon. It left everyone guessing and Matron kept giving hints like: "We will be getting new theatre gowns." What on earth we would need them for, nobody knew. Somewhere around the middle of the year, the day arrived for the big surprise, and everyone was introduced to a new doctor. Our little Doctor Stevenson was gone and was replaced with a new doctor—a tall, dark man, probably in his mid-thirties. No wonder there had to be new theatre gowns made to fit him. I was on a late shift that day, so I was not there at the initial introduction, but after I came on duty I had to go to the office where all the patient charts were kept. I knocked on the door and asked to do the charts, but as I turned to go out of the room, the new doctor, who had been standing by the fireplace, took his stethoscope and wacked me across the behind with it saying: "Hey you, you're the only one I haven't caught up with yet." Matron Catford introduced me. Wouldn't you know it. I blushed so deeply, I felt my face burn, said "how do you do?" and went for my life.

Thus started a game that finally taught me how to handle

my shyness and stood me in good stead for the rest of my life. Every time I'd meet him when there were no patients or public around, he'd say, "come on, blush for me," and I would. That went on for a long time, but I gradually found it didn't bother me anymore.

My confidence was growing. Towards the end of my training in Booleroo Centre we had a new nurse, Christine. She was very young, having started at fifteen. Her mother was a trained nurse and so Christine had been briefed about how to behave. On one of her first days with us, I had her in my care. We were standing at the table in the courtyard preparing stock to be sterilised. Suddenly a man appeared behind us. He put his arm around my waist and said, "come on, blush for me."

"Go away!" I immediately responded. "I'm not blushing for you or anyone else!"

With that he turned and walked off to the office.

"Who was that?" a wide-eyed Christine asked.

"Oh," I said. "That's the doctor."

Chris couldn't believe her eyes. This was certainly not the way her mother had taught her to behave towards a doctor.

But it seemed my blushing had stopped, not only with the doctor, but with everyone.

ONE OF THE other sisters we had was a very nice person, but very lazy. She used to walk around, stopping to talk to patients, and demanding that the other nurses do tasks while she watched on. When the weather turned cold and we had to have fires going in all the rooms, one of her habits was to go into a room where nurses were working and stand there, talking and directing the nurses, while she warmed her backside in front of the fire. On one occasion there were two of us making the rooms ready for the patients' return to bed. There were eight beds in the women's ward, so Sister was there warming herself for some time. Suddenly we could smell material burning. Smoke coming from behind the sister as she'd got too close to the fire and was starting to smoulder. Everyone yelled and screamed and got water to throw on her, but the fire was out very quickly. The worse she got was a uniform with no bottom in it—and she was cured of the habit of standing in front of the fire all day.

Another sister we had, who arrived towards the end of my time at Booleroo Hospital, was a nice lady, but she had this terrible habit of lying. She would not take responsibility for anything that went wrong but always found someone to blame. On one occasion during surgery, we didn't have a second doctor as we usually did. It was a tonsillectomy, and I was the scrub nurse. This meant I was not to handle anything except the equipment that had already been sterilised. This sister was to do the anaesthetic, which involved putting a mask over the patient's face and slowly dropping ether into the mask until they went to sleep. Because of this method it was possible to leave the patient briefly if necessary, so Sister could scully (be available for any incidental tasks), if needed. While I was getting the patient ready, Sister set up the theatre, then I had to scrub and be ready to assist Doctor. We started the operation, and all was going smoothly until I went to hand Doctor an instrument, and it was not there. Sister should have checked all the instruments before the operation as part of her set up, but I looked everywhere and it wasn't there. Sister insisted she'd put it on the table and it must be my fault that I couldn't find it. But Doctor sent another nurse to see if there was another one in the disinfectant. Sure enough, they were all there, which meant Sister had not put the instruments out in the first place. Still, she insisted it was my fault and I must have knocked it off the table.

It was well known that Sister believed she only had to go to confession, and it was alright if she had lied.

On another occasion, at Christmas, Doctor Wheaton had invited all the staff to a party—probably the only party we were ever invited to—and he allowed Sister to drive us nurses home in his car. As we drove away from his place, one of the Western Australian girls asked if she could drive the car. She had no licence and had never driven a car in her life, but she put on such a to-do that Sister said "okay" and let her drive. When we got to the crossroads at the hotel corner, she was going too fast and forgot to take her foot off the accelerator. Next thing we knew, she had mounted the curb of the medium strip and ran into the fence around the war memorial. There was a pipe along the top of the fence and as the car hit, it broke and went straight through the windscreen. It was amazing that one of us in the back wasn't skewered. The police had to be called, and the doctor whose car had just been wrecked. Although it was wrong of the young nurse to be driving the car, still Sister tried to blame the rest of us for the accident. That is why there is now no fence around the war memorial at Booleroo Centre. And sadly, because of her behaviour, that was how I remember that sister.

Doctor Wheaton would have been very cross if we ever tried to play a joke on him, but he loved playing jokes on everyone else. Once, when we day staff arrived early in the morning, Matron said a person had been admitted during the night with a very unusual case. She told us to go in to see the patient and observe everything we could about her. At the time there were not a lot of patients in the hospital and the general ward didn't have anyone else in it. We were still instructed to be very quiet as any sudden movement might do the patient a lot of harm. "Don't all go in at the same time," the matron told us. "Too many people could be very distressing to her."

Obediently, one by one, we went in to inspect the patient. I was the last to go in and by that time I suspected there was mischief afoot, just from the reaction of the other staff. Sure enough, as I approached the bed I could see very strange hair poking out. And there she was. A mop, propped up in bed and made to look like a person's head. A sheet of paper was pinned on top of the bedclothes, filled in as patient's records. Her name was Miss Phoebe Mopp and time of admission was DOA (dead on arrival). Doctor, Matron and Sister had positioned themselves in a spot where they could watch our reaction—they didn't get much of a laugh out of me but I did give a bit of a smile.

On another occasion, Matron sent in an order for one dozen measuring spoons, the kind that had a teaspoon size at one end and a tablespoon size at the other. They were used for measuring powders in the medicine area or measuring baby food if there was a sick baby. When the spoons arrived she hadn't ordered a dozen spoons, she'd ordered a dozen *packets* of spoons, and each one had twelve spoons in it. She couldn't believe the mistake, but they could not be returned, and so they were stacked in the medicine cupboard in hopes they'd be used over the next few years. I was in the sterilisation room, where we did a lot of our work, when Dr Wheaton came in.

"Can you get into the medicine cupboard and get me a couple packets of spoons," he asked. "And don't let Matron know about it."

I was now in my senior year and allowed to get things from the locked cupboard. I went to the office when I was sure Matron would be either busy or having morning tea and asked if I could have the keys on some pretext. I quickly removed the spoons and returned the keys, then later Doctor came and got them. I didn't ask what he wanted them for but soon found out. He and Sister Selor went to Matron's flat and began putting them into everything they could. When Matron came off duty she changed out of her uniform and every bit of clothing had a spoon in it. She was going out to dinner, and as she was leaving Sister Selor helped her on with her coat, and slipped a spoon in each pocket. When Matron came home that night she prepared for bed and spoons fell out of her pyjamas. She got her hot water bottle and when she put her feet on it she felt a lump under the cover—another spoon. During the night she had to go to the loo, which in those days was a chamber pot under the bed, and when she had finished, she heard the clink of a spoon floating. The next morning, we had scrambled eggs for breakfast, and Sister Selor came in early and got us to help lift Matron's serve of eggs while she popped a spoon beneath. When Matron came in, we all sat down and as she lifted her knife and fork she said "If I see another spoon I'll scream." And with that she cut into the eggs. She didn't scream, but we all knew that it was the end of the joke.

Although we had our share of laughter there were times of sadness. These were often hard to handle, and most of the girls would turn to cigarettes to relieve the stress. I never used them and although they tried to convince me that they helped, I never could see the sense in all that money going up in smoke. I seemed to be able to handle the stress okay with the help of my family, but the experiences were still hard.

One such terrible time was when a little boy from a nearby town was brought into the hospital by his parents. He was dressed only in a pair of shorts, a thin shirt and sandals on his feet, and was very very sick. He was suffering from starvation and had Ricketts. When he came to us we couldn't get him to eat anything except peanut paste on bread, and we had to work hard to get food into him to help fight the disease. He was such a beautiful child and all the staff fell in love with him. The parents hadn't brought anything for him and apparently weren't going to bring him anything, so the staff did what they could to make up for it. One of the sisters went down to the local general store, Prests, and bought him some pyjamas, a dressing gown and some slippers, and another nurse bought him some books and toys. All the staff loved to play with him when they were off duty and were delighted as we coaxed him to eat the right diet. Soon he began to fill out and eat well. Everyone was on the lookout to get him a new toy or book, and as he was gradually allowed to be up and around, they bought him clothes. After some weeks he was looking healthy, and so he was discharged. When his father came to get him and saw all his new gear being packed up, he said, "He won't be being so well treated at home." And never a truer word was said. I don't remember how long it was, but only weeks later he was rushed to hospital, and here we found our dear little friend, white and limp and very sick. By the time the night was out he had gone to be with the Lord. We were all stunned and no one could believe he could have deteriorated that quickly. When he was re-admitted he was dressed in the same ragged clothes as before. It broke our hearts.

Another case I had to help with was a man who was brought in with the DTs (the delirium tremens, or dangerous symptoms of alcohol withdrawal). He had obviously done nothing but drink, was filthy from head to toe and his clothes looked as if they hadn't been washed for months. He was brought into the hospital at the beginning of the night and it fell to me and one other nurse to deal with him. He was put in the old men's sleep-out which was rarely used but was made up in case of emergency. In this case because he was so drunk he was quite rowdy. We had to strip him down and get him scrubbed, and into some hospital pyjamas. But before we could get the clean clothes on him, we had to literally scrub the dirt from his skin. His toenails had grown so long they had started to curl around his toes and it was difficult to cut them back to a reasonable size. The poor old man kept yelling at us to leave him alone and every now and then he would say, "You're killing me you girls, I'll be home in the morning." We finally got him all cleaned up and Doctor gave him something to calm him down and give him some sleep. However, when we came on duty the next day, we learned he had died during the night. We felt very sad. And indeed, he was going home, as apparently part of his property took in the cemetery of his home town.

Then there was the first experience I had with Catholic people. In those years, there was a great divide between Protestants and Catholics which was ingrained in our society. But I soon learned they are great people who live their lives just as we did. There were a few things about their understanding of the Christian faith that differed from mine, and that's okay, we all have a right to our opinion. But sometimes my views clashed, such as Sister Banks' idea that as long as she went to confession she could lie as much as she wanted to. Another belief I couldn't quite go along with was how people believed if they didn't do as the Priest said, they would be damned. On one occasion I was nursing a lady from another town. She told me her story. When she was young, she'd been a staunch Catholic, and then she met the man she was going to marry. They were happy and loved each other dearly but when she told the family they were going to get married, everything fell apart. He was a Protestant. The Priest was called and she was told that she did not have permission from the Church to marry outside her faith. She fought and fought and said she was determined to marry the man she loved. The Priest insisted that the Catholic Church would not recognise the marriage and, therefore, she would be living in sin. It made no difference. They went ahead and got married and were still married and happy up to the time I was talking to her and until they died, as far as I know. But just before the wedding the Priest visited her one last time and he told her that because she would not do as he said, their marriage would be cursed, they would never have children, and she would be cursed with snakes for the rest of her life. She was terrified of snakes and indeed, both her baby boys died right after their birth. This incident was one I couldn't understand, it didn't show the love of Christ in any way.

When you're a nurse in the local hospital of your area, you found that most patients were people you knew. That was fine when everything went well, but sometimes it didn't. I had started to go out with one of the boys from the Wirrabara area. We'd only been to a couple of dances—all the nurses and their boyfriends regularly got together to go to whatever shindig was on. On this occasion I was on night duty when there was an urgent call to prepare two beds for an accident that was coming in from Wirrabara. We swung into action getting ready for the admissions. However, when they arrived, I was horrified to find that one of them had been fatally injured and didn't make it to the hospital. Then my heart sank when they told me it was my friend. He and another man had been approaching Wirrabara, going down the hill into the town too fast. The driver lost control on the bend in the road, flipping the vehicle over and over down the hill. He survived the crash but was very smashed up and struggled to breathe all night. He eventually lost the fight in the morning.

These kinds of things were very hard to handle, but we learned to get on with the job, as the work had to be done.

Happily, there were things to distract us. Once, when we were feeling bored, someone suggested we see if we could get some of the soldiers from the El Alamein army camp, near Port Augusta, over for the day. One of the girls had a relative who was there, so she rang and asked for him about coming over to Booleroo. There were three of them who thought that would be a good idea. The arrangements were made, and over they came. There were three of us nurses who were either on night duty or had a day off, and even though the boys didn't get there until lunch time, it still gave us a good few hours until they had to head home to be in camp. We had a lovely day taking them all around the place and then we waved goodbye as they headed back to camp, never to be seen again.

We spent our time-off getting away from the hospital as much as we could. Each of us nurses got to know the local lads around the place. I made a connection with a young man named Merve who worked as a sawyer in the Wirrabara Forest. Merve became my special partner in all non-nursing activities, until he left his job in the Wirrabara Forest to go to my brother's station at Wilkatana. He wasn't there long—one day the other workers went to look for him, but he had gone, and we never heard from him again. Even without Merve, I enjoyed the social life. We always went to events as a group, the young lads providing us with transport. There were plenty of dances on during the middle of the year. Every town took their turn in having a Saturday night dance and they also had special nights (usually Wednesday night) for the big balls.

When we went to the Saturday night dances, we'd dress up in ballerina length dresses, all very colourful and usually with lots of tulle or flared skirts. The Saturday night dance always ended with the National Anthem on the dot of twelve o'clock, almost like the Cinderella story. The reason it stopped at midnight—it was considered morally wrong to be dancing on a Sunday. However, on the Wednesday night balls, the dancing continued until 1am. We were far more dressed up for these evenings wearing full length ball gowns. I even had a fox-fur stole for some of the gowns and a white fur jacket for the others, and of course you didn't go to a ball without long gloves. They needed to be right up to the elbow.

One of the bands that used to play for the dances was the AJ Hot Five. The band was made up of the young people I had worked with before I went nursing—Pat Redding from the bakery was the MC, and he always made sure we had a grand entrance. As soon as we arrived, they would play the tune to the war time song, *Nursie, come over here and hold my hand*, altering the words to fit the tempo of the dance they were playing at the time. I remember that whenever AJ Hot Five were playing, they had a huge light in the shape of a new moon which they hung in each hall, and whenever they played a modern waltz or fox-trot, they turned out all the lights so there was only the light of the big new moon. It was all very romantic.

The biggest occasion was the hospital ball, held every year, and when it was on, it was all hands on deck. The Hospital Auxiliary ladies worked hard to do the cooking and decorating of the hall, but the nurses had to make the streamers to hang from the ceiling. When we came on duty, we'd each be given two different rolls of coloured crepe paper and had to turn them into plaits. We carried the rolls around in our pockets, and in any quiet moment on shift, we had to take them out and continue to plait the streamers. When the big day came there was a lot of excitement amongst the staff. We always hoped we wouldn't be one of the two unlucky girls appointed to stay on duty until 10.30pm. The dancing always started right at 8pm giving the night staff a chance to go to the ball for a couple of hours, then they came back to the hospital and the other two would go off for the rest of the evening. The doctor always held a pre-ball party attended by the senior staff, and the Secretary of the Board also held a party, so none of them arrived at the ball until at least 9.30pm. When they arrived, everything would stop while they entered and they would take their seats right at the top of the hall in front of the stage. They didn't mix with the nursing staff, except for Mr Bob, who always danced one dance with each nurse.

Dances and balls were great nights of entertainment. The law at that time didn't allow alcohol in the halls and this meant if anyone wanted to drink, they had to go 300 yards down the road and sit in their car. The majority of people stayed in the hall for most of the time, and they all danced. Even with the liquor laws it didn't stop some of the nurses going out and getting drunk in the evening. They still had to report in to the night staff, and they'd often have to be put to bed if they were too much the worse for wear.

Later on, well after I was married, the laws were changed and they were allowed to have a liquor licence. This brought in the era of what they called the cabarets. The dances were still held in the hall but there were small tables and chairs placed around the edges, and so people would come to the dance and sit and drink at the tables, and didn't bother so much about dancing. Sadly, it wasn't long before the whole skill of ballroom dancing disappeared.

. . .

Before the hospital came into being, more than 100 years ago, the building used to be the old police station and jail. The modern building expanded far beyond the original jail which was only the southern end of the hospital. There wasn't much evidence of the jail left, except when you went out the back door leading to the laundry and nurses' home. This door was bigger than usual and very thick, with a small window which had been covered over with a piece of tin. It had a huge bolt to keep it closed, and it could only be opened from the inside. This was the door we nurses had to go through after our shifts to get back to the home. There was a legend that said the door could never be locked, and although many a nurse made sure it was locked every night, it was always open in the morning.

That whole end of the hospital was very dark, painted in brown colours. It consisted of the equivalent of three rooms down each side of a passage which went from the front of the building to the back, and the rooms were tiny. The passage only had one light, so it was very dark, and it was so narrow you could stand in the middle of it and stretch out your arms and touch the walls on both sides. On one side of the passage there was a double private room, but this rarely got used. It was used as the last resort when we were very full. Next to that was the maternity theatre, or mid ward as we called it. This consisted of a tiny room with one bed and a cupboard down one wall. The opposite wall had a window in it, with trollies lined along it. At the foot of the bed was the sink for the Doctor to scrub, but there was so little room that when there was anyone at the sink no one could get past to the other side of the bed. When a woman was in labour, all the necessary staff had to get into position in the room and only the last one in could leave the room to get anything or do anything outside.

Next to the mid ward was the nursery, though the rooms were not connected and could only be reached by going through the dark passage and out through the closed-in veranda. This veranda had a small room at one end and a cellar at the other, with the big jail door in the middle. It's strange to think of such a dingy, uninviting place being for the newborns, but that was the way things were arranged. On the other side of the passage was the front office, the out-patients room which was actually a wide passage that had been closed off, and the sterilizing room where we did all our other tasks including sterilising the stock. The whole area was very spooky at night.

One night we had a real fright. The hospital front doors were never locked, so anyone could come in at any time, but it was never a worry as people could be trusted. At night, once the work was done and the patients were settled, the nurses would go into the office or the sterilising room and continue to do tasks that didn't disturb the sleeping patients.

On this occasion there had been a ball at Booleroo and, as usual, all the nurses had gone off for the night except for me and a fellow unlucky nurse. There had been a relieving doctor at the hospital as Doctor Wheaton was away for a trip —most unusual as he rarely left the place. His temporary replacement was a very young doctor who'd only just finished his training, but he'd taken the opportunity to get some experience in the country. That night, the other young nurse on duty with me was very nervous, and when we were sitting in the office attending to things, she kept a fire poker close by in case she should be attacked. No one thought for a moment there would be any kind of trouble in little old Booleroo. It was the job of the senior nurse on duty to attend to any babies that needed a nappy change during the night, and sometimes it was necessary to top the bottles up with a little bit of boiled water rather than wake their mother. That was the case on this night. My colleague was sitting in the office armchair with her poker over her shoulder, and I was feeding some water to the one and only baby from the nursery, when we suddenly heard a very loud and regular thumping sound. It was coming from the back of the hospital and up along the very dark passage towards the office. We both froze and stared at the door. The doorknob started to turn, accompanied by several strange noises. As the door opened, I clutched the baby close to me and got up to run, following the other girl who had screamed, dropped her poker, and was well in front of me. We tore into the darkness and ran for dear life, not stopping until we'd gotten to the other side of the courtyard, into the passage that had the private rooms, and into the men's ward. I then gingerly peeked out of the passage only to find the doctor and three other nurses hot-footing it over to us calling, "it's alright, it's only us." They had just been playing a prank on us. We both felt rather stupid, but the nurse with me was so terrified she almost collapsed. When someone finally took the poor baby from me I also felt very shaky. The joke had gone very wrong and although I managed to pull myself together to finish my work, the other girl had to be sent off duty and given medication to calm her down and get her to sleep.

Not long after, when two other night staff girls were in the office, they heard the front door open. There was no mistaking it, as it had a very distinctive sound—first the wire door then the big door. They waited for a visitor to come in but no one came. They went out to the hospital area but there was no sign of anyone. The front door was shut but the back door (with the big bolt) was open. This made them very nervous, but they convinced themselves they must have misheard it. However, the next night at about the same time, around 2am, it happened again. Once again, the front door was closed but the back door was open. They reported it to the Matron but she told them not to be silly, as it was only their imagination after all the shenanigans from the prank.

Then there was a change of night staff and the new staff had the same experience. They were quite sure someone had come into the waiting room and gone out by the back door. Again they complained to the Matron so she spoke to the Secretary of the Board, but his response was the same. It was all imagination. By now we nurses decided that we would have to do something ourselves to help our colleagues. We made a plan that we would set our alarms for 1am and all go over to the hospital for an hour and wait quietly. If the perpetrator did come in, we'd be ready to descend on him, knock him to the ground and sit on him. Meanwhile, one nurse would administer an injection of paraldehyde which would knock him out, and another designated nurse would go for help. We thought it was a good plan, and pity help anyone who came uninvited. But although we put the plan into action, no one came, and though we strained our ears, no one heard the front door. We were disappointed.

But the story didn't end there. A night or so later, at 1am, it was necessary to ring the visiting doctor to come to the hospital for another matter. He came immediately in Doctor Wheaton's little Morris Minor. The car had no muffler and could be heard when he left the doctor's house. As he turned the corner and approached the hospital, he saw a man walking along the footpath. Just as the doctor pulled up, the man jumped the fence of the hospital grounds and ran towards the nurses' home. The doctor took after him. The stranger headed straight up the alleyway between the hospital and nurses' home and then disappeared into the darkness. At last, we nurses had our proof. There was a kerfuffle as the police were called and the board were suddenly quite concerned. After that, they decided to have some kind of lock on the front door after all. There was quite an investigation, but no one was apprehended. There had been a gang of painters from the Riverland staying in an old cottage next to the hospital. It was interesting that they left the district the next day, and we never had any trouble from that day on.

By this time, I'd finished my two years and eight months of training at the Booleroo Centre District Hospital—well beyond the one month my brother predicted. Now it was time for me to go to the Royal Adelaide Hospital to continue my training. Even though there was a lot of excitement about my going off to the city, it was a time of sadness, as I had to leave everything that had become familiar around me. I had learned my craft well in that environment, and I was going to miss it.

If my brother had predicted I wouldn't last long in this next venture, this time I may have agreed what was to come would be too much for me, so I should just stay at home, thank you. But true to the training of my parents, when you start a thing, you are responsible to finish it. So I set off for my time in Adelaide.

10

THE ROYAL ADELAIDE HOSPITAL

I don't recall much about arriving in Adelaide and getting started at the RAH, but there are a few things that stand out. I went to board with my Auntie Ollie and Uncle Wal. Wilmington was too far to drive home when I had time off.

Once again, I found I was on my own. Usually new nurses start in a group, so they have the support of each other to learn the ropes. However, when I started, there was only one other new girl. She was a migrant who had already partly trained in her own country but now had to retrain. Unfortunately, I didn't get to know her at all after our first meeting.

Instead of being with a group of girls sent together to the different wards as our training progressed, in those first few weeks I was always on my own. I found this difficult. I was still very shy, and even though it didn't affect me in the same way it once did, I still found it difficult to get to know new people. As part of training, everyone was changed around every six weeks. Thankfully over time, as I approached each new ward, I found several of the same girls, and so it wasn't long before I made friends with some of them.

It was a big adjustment. Although I had been senior nurse at Booleroo Centre, I was only counted as a second-year trainee at the Royal Adelaide. In many ways it felt like I was starting over.

The first ward I was sent to was Light Ward. It was by the edge of the Botanic Gardens next door to the hospital. When I'd finished my first day, I was walking across the grounds and I heard a yell coming from the floor above. On that floor dwelt that mass of humanity called the 'housies'—the young doctors who had finished their training but were lucky enough to be accepted for a year's experience at the RAH. When I looked up, there was the young doctor who had scared the daylights out of us with his prank in the old jail part of the Booleroo Hospital. There he was, waving to me.

"I see you are here!" he called. "What ward are you on?"

"Light Ward!" I called back.

"Oh, you poor thing. I'll see you around." There the conversation ended.

I never saw him again.

Compared to Booleroo Hospital, the Royal Adelaide was enormous—spread across three locations. As part of our training, we had to do a stint at the main location on North Terrace, at the Hampstead Wards working with infectious diseases, and at Magill, which was partly for patients to recuperate between operations, and partly palliative care for cancer patients.

I started at North Terrace first. We did not have fixed living quarters, but were given whichever room was spare at the time, depending on which ward we were working on. The only exception was if we were unwell ourselves. Then we were set up in a small ward named Light Sick Nurses. I had the pleasure (or otherwise) of both working there and being a patient there. The nurses had to prepare meals for their sick colleagues and I remember being taught by one of the other girls how to make the most delicious omelette that I've never been able to get right since.

I spent most of my time in Light Ward. It was a men's medical, with fifty beds. When we came on duty, we were allotted a section of six or seven beds, though one of us would be scheduled to be on hand to assist any nurse who needed help with a patient. The Charge Sister was a very senior nurse named Sister Jess Ford, but we all called her Jess —behind her back of course. Everyone was frightened of Sister Ford as she ran a strict ward. She told everyone exactly what their job was, and you did as you were told. She was so particular about small things. When you were assigned your corner of seven, you had until the next day to know all the patients' names and everything about them that was written on their chart. All the beds in your corner had to be made by the time the doctor did his rounds. Sister Ford was very particular about this. Making the bed meant envelope corners on all the beds, with the envelope opening facing away from the door, the pillows plumped up, and the little wheel at the end of the bed turned to the side and facing the door. At no time did you do anything that had not been ordered by Sister Ford.

On one occasion one of the doctors was seeing a patient and Jess was not in the room. He came to me and told me to give the patient an injection, and as I had been doing that kind of thing since my time in Booleroo, it was no effort. But when Jess found out, I was in big trouble. It was not my job, she scolded me. The dressing nurse should have been the one to do it! I didn't make a mistake like that again and made sure I followed the strict protocol from then on.

I learned quite a long time later that there were a certain group of senior sisters who insisted they choose their own staff for their wards. They nearly always chose country transfers as they considered them the best trained nurses. Jess, being deputy Matron, had first choice. To be working in her ward put you in the top class. Which is wonderful praise, even though I had the audacity to give an injection by myself.

It was while I was in Light Ward that I met Janet Eddison-Waters, and we became friendly. Janet was a bright young lady from the southeast of the state but her surname was a mouthful for the charge sisters and doctors who always referred to us by our last names. She was engaged to be married though, and whenever "Eddison-Waters" was called, she would huff and say, "the sooner it's Smith, the better."

Janet was always on the lookout for anyone she could influence to get involved with Christian things. This was a big help to me as I had no church to go to in Adelaide. There was a chapel on the hospital grounds with a service held every Sunday by a different denomination. It made no difference to me if it was Methodist or Lutheran, although the Catholics preferred not to have a protestant in the congregation. I usually turned up on a Sunday for the service, when I could.

During our second year at the Royal Adelaide, Janet and I were on night duty together. The night staff were bused to a beautiful old home on the large grounds out on Kensington Road. This is where we were housed for the duration of our night duties. We often went out on the lawns in the nice weather and Janet saw her chance to do a bit of evangelising. It wasn't long and we had a nice little Bible study going under the shade of the beautiful big trees on the grounds.

One new nurse who Janet enticed into her group was a girl who came from a religion we didn't understand. She was a very quiet and shy young girl and although we all roomed together, she never spent any of her time off with us. Her father was always waiting at the door when she had a day off. She never joined us for extra times in which we would go into the city to do a little shopping. She had long hair which was kept plaited with the plaits wound around her head. When Janet invited this young lady to come to our Bible study we realised she was very religious. When Janet asked her to say a word of thanks after our meeting she said, "I don't know where in the book to find that." Everyone was surprised and the poor girl embarrassed. On another occasion we asked her to join us up on the roof patio of the nurses home where some of the girls went to sunbake. We intended to sunbake but do our Bible study at the same time. We all came out in our shorts and skimpy tops with sunglasses and hats. Because it was the top of the nurses' home, we knew we wouldn't be seen by anyone other than a low flying aircraft. This girl came in full uniform including a cape. Apparently, she was not allowed to go anywhere public without her cape. Unfortunately, we didn't share a night shift after that, so I'm not sure what happened to her.

While I was working in Light Ward, I experienced a man suffering from kidney failure. This was back in the days when there was no such thing as dialysis and so the poor things just had to ride it out until they died. This man was far advanced in the kidney failure and suffered terrible agony. The fluid continued to build up and his skin stretched tight over his body. We tried to relieve the pain as best we could but it was of little value. Every time he'd have an injection, his skin would split when the needle went in because it was so tight. It is something you just don't forget. Thankfully dialysis came into existence during the time I was at the RAH, though there was only one machine and it wasn't at the

Royal Adelaide. The single dialysis machine was down at the Queen Elizabeth Hospital, Woodville, late in 1959.

Below Light Ward was Flinders Ward, which had a small area at one end where they put any tetanus patients. It had two rooms, one room was soundproofed. We were instructed that when you worked in there you were not to make any noise at all—any small sound could kill a patient, even a whisper. I only had to work there once thankfully, but it was an experience.

Soon it was my turn to spend time at the wards out at Magill. There were three buildings, each with four wards. One was women's rest and rehabilitation, one for men's rest and rehabilitation, and one was palliative care for cancer patients. I was lucky enough to be put into the men's ward. The patients in this ward were men who'd had surgery or some other treatment but couldn't be sent home until some follow up procedure. On the whole they were not very sick, so the nursing wasn't hard and in fact we had a lot of fun there.

But, once again I was sent out on my own. I was waiting for the bus to Magill when a girl came up to me and said, "Are you going out to Magill Wards?"

"Yes," I answered.

With that she threw a neat bundle of clothing at me. "Will you take this with you? I have to do some shopping before I go out."

"Okay," I said, "but how will I find you when I get out there?"

"Don't worry," she said. "I'll find you."

And off she went.

I was worried that I'd never find the girl as I didn't know my way around the new place. When I was allotted my sleeping quarters, it was in a long building with a passage down the middle. I was sitting in the room sorting out my things when there was a knock on the door. When it opened, in came the girl who had asked me to bring her laundry. I couldn't believe it when she told me she was to room right across the passage from me. Her name was Janet McFarlane, and she became a very good friend. We remained friends the rest of our lives—even my children later called her Auntie Jan.

We had quite a few interesting cases on the Magill Men's Ward. One man had his arm removed, and he complained that the fingers of his lost arm itched. Of course the poor man was nearly driven mad because there was no hand for him to scratch. We had another man who'd had back surgery and couldn't walk without sticks. He had to keep exercising daily trying to get things going again. He had a wooden structure like a path with rails along the side that he could hold, lean, or just balance with. Then there was the very young, very good looking, man who came from the South-East somewhere. He'd been trying to get a tractor out of a bog and got the leg of his trousers caught under the spinning back wheel, pulling his leg into it. It had ripped all the flesh off his lower leg but luckily no broken bones. He had to have his leg dressed every six hours and I could see how the new flesh was gradually growing over the injury from the side inward. I loved doing dressings and this one in particular because it was so interesting to watch the leg repair itself. He had to return to the RAH from time to time to have more skin grafts and then back to Magill for us to keep the wound open and allow the new flesh to grow.

Another patient was a sailor from a foreign ship. He was a wild looking man. Most of us were very nervous around him. He was short and dark in colouring and had intense eyes, and when he smiled he showed a row of silver-filled teeth and a lot of decay. He used to get out of bed and wander around the place, and you never knew where he would turn up. When I was on night duty, we had to do our bookwork at the office desk which looked out over the grounds. At night it was scary but I aways liked to have the blind up as I didn't like not knowing what was going on outside. One night we were working and I was looking out the window and saw there was someone walking around the grounds in the dark. It frightened the life out of us. Then we discovered the sailor was missing, not only from his bed but the whole building, so we had to find him. Eventually we did find him. It was him who'd been walking around the grounds. We were all pleased to see him go.

It was while I was at the Magill Wards that I first came in contact with the game of baseball. It was played every Wednesday night and the grounds were not far from the hospital. Jan McFarlane was going out with a young policeman, Ron Marsh, and so when there was baseball on, he would turn up in his little car and take us to the game. It was winter and freezing in the stand watching the play. My feet used to get so cold I thought my toes would drop off. Then one day we thought we'd try an experiment. We reckoned that having your feet squashed into a shoe would not allow the blood to circulate properly and, therefore, if the toes were freed, would help to keep them warm. Stupid? I'm not so sure. We decided to give it a go, so I put on a pair of sandals with no socks to inhibit the movement and off we went to the baseball. Strangely enough my feet were not anywhere near as cold as usual that night. Did the experiment work or was it just the power of suggestion? Who knows?

Ron had a friend named Bob, who used to accompany us to the baseball games. Over time we became quite friendly;

he became my boyfriend for a few months, but I soon realised it wasn't going anywhere, so the relationship didn't continue.

Not long after that I met another boy, also named Bob. He was a young man from Adelaide, and when I had time off, he'd come and pick me up from Aunty Ol's. I'd accompany him while he worked, driving around Adelaide to fill up the peanut machines in the billiard halls.

Bob had an MG car—the classiest car for young people of the time—and we'd drive from one billiard hall to another. I'd sit in the car because women weren't allowed in the billiard halls in those days, and he'd hop inside and fill up the peanut machines.

"You wait," he used to say to me. "In days to come, I'm going to be the Peanut King of Australia. You'll run into me in the future and say, 'I used to know this bloke, now he's the Peanut King.'"

Our relationship didn't continue long after that. I have no idea if he became the Peanut King, in Australia or otherwise, but hopefully he was able to follow his dream.

WE WORKED our way through the days at the Magill Wards and were soon sent back to North Terrace RAH to continue. When I had another stint on night duty, I was put into a block of four wards known as the Floor Wards. My job was to be the extra nurse for the four wards, and therefore I was called from ward to ward whenever the staff needed an extra hand. The staff in each ward were allowed a break once during the night and were supplied with their tea and biscuits—always milk-coffee biscuits—we nurses were sure the hospital had shares in the coffee biscuit factory. In one of the wards, the sister used to keep a supply of the better type of sweet biscuits that she gave to the doctors for their morning tea. These were kept in a locked cupboard and no one dared touch them. The girls on that floor all complained about her and her biscuits and how unfair it was that we never got anything but coffee biscuits. They would look at the lock on the cupboard and announce that if they could only break in, they'd have a feast. I'm not sure what came over me but one night I commented that I could open the cupboard. They couldn't believe it and challenged me to do it. I studied the padlock and could see it wasn't a good one. I got out my nailfile, slipped the point down beside the lock, then lifted it, and to my surprise, it sprang open. I left the girls to it then, and went off to the work I had to do. The next day I was moved to another ward but I heard that they ate the biscuits and locked the cupboard again. Apparently, the poor sister was beside herself when she found she didn't have special biscuits for the doctors, but she couldn't do anything about it as she wasn't supposed to be giving the biscuits to the doctors in the first place.

Another experience I had on the Floor Wards happened once again on night duty. Usually, beds in the wards are all close to each other but in this ward, most beds were close, then there was a gap for a door, and then another bed. On this night, the patient in the separate bed was a lady who was very restless. She was positioned just across from the staff desk, so I could easily see what was happening without having to leave the desk. When the restlessness persisted, I went and sat alongside and asked if there was anything wrong. In a low whisper she told me she was terrified of the surgery scheduled for the next day. It was a small procedure which was to sever a nerve in her head. The purpose was to change a certain part of her personality, because she had been bombarded with suicidal thoughts. When it came down to it, she told me she'd been born a catholic but had chosen to marry a protestant, and since then had started having terrible thoughts that led her to try to take her life. Although she hadn't asked for it, the priest had been in to see her that day and told her she had to have communion with him before the operation or God would see to it that she would die. She had refused as she wanted nothing to do with the catholic church, but after the priest left, the other catholic patients in the ward were constantly trying to change her mind. Here I was with all the facts but no idea what I was talking about, assuring her that God would not do that kind of thing and that I would see to it that the pestering from the other patients would stop. In the early hours of the morning, I watched carefully and sure enough, a few patients were following wherever she went. In this ward the patients where all ambulant and so it was easy for them to gang up on her. I also followed wherever she went, and made sure they could not get at her. By the time I had to go off duty she was prepared for surgery and there were too many nurses around for the other patients to get up to their mischief. I went and visited this patient in my own time after her operation. She had been moved into another surgical ward, and was grateful and agreed I was right. God had looked after her.

I SPENT a period of time in these wards on day duty as well. In one of the wards the sister had a habit of losing her temper. The slightest little thing would make her furious and she would literally scream at the poor nurse who was in trouble. She'd grab her glasses on both sides and squeeze them together, shaking them furiously as she screamed, "You bloody girls I'll kill you!" It was most off putting, to say nothing of the many pairs of glasses she broke, but none of the senior staff seemed to worry about it.

In this ward there was a young girl who'd been unconscious for many months. She had been taken to a dance by her father and on the way home he'd stopped to post a letter. While he was out of the car, a drunk driver had come along the street and swerved, hitting the car, and leaving this young girl unconscious. Because she was only being kept alive on life support, she had withered away to almost a skeleton. It was so sad to see.

In another ward I was on duty when it was "take night"—the day or night that new patients were admitted. A young man was brought in, and I was told to see if I could clean him up before he went to surgery. When I approached the bed, I was horrified to find the man was covered in blood. I prepared a bowl of water, soap, and towels, and then he said to me in a weeping voice, "I'm so sorry, nurse, I'm so sorry to put you through this." It was then I discovered that the blood came from his scrotum. He'd mutilated it with a razor blade in a suicide attempt and because it has a high source of blood, there was blood everywhere. I wasn't quite sure how I was going to get him cleaned up and was thankful when the surgeon appeared beside the bed and said, "don't worry about it nurse, we'll clean it up in the theatre." Whew. Was I glad about that.

It was while I was working in these Floor Wards that I was coming to the end of my training and I well remember one old man. I don't remember why he was in hospital but he was a bright fellow and appreciated everything we did for him. Every day at visiting time he'd be sitting up in bed, doing nothing and saying nothing, with two visitors, one on each side of the bed. These two women spent the whole time sniping at each other, as nasty as can be, while he just sat and looked peacefully on. It turned out one of the women was his wife, and the other was his girlfriend, and they all lived together in one home. And yet the day I was leaving he said to me, "can I give you some advice on marriage?"

"Yes," said I.

"Well," he ventured "Always remember, no matter what has happened during the day, never let the sun go down on your anger." Strange advice from one who was in his position, but perhaps that was how he managed to live with these two bickering women and yet remained serene.

Even though theatre was my favourite place to work, I didn't get the chance to be sent there while at the RAH. Instead I was sent to the gynaecological theatre, which I also enjoyed. It was in an old building and because it was only gynaecological work, it was small compared to the other theatres, but the sister in charge was really great. There was only her and staff nurse besides the nursing staff, so it was almost like being back at Booleroo. The main honorary surgeon was Doctor Bright, and everyone was frightened of him, except the sister who stood up to him and had him under control. We nurses all felt safe with her. If he dared to say anything or criticize our work she would tell him in no uncertain terms that the nurses were her responsibility, and he had no say in it. I suspect they knew each other very well and were really good friends, but being true professionals, you wouldn't really know.

The medical students used to come into the theatre when there was an operation going on, and they would perch on the benches along the wall at the foot of the operating table. From there Doctor Bright would do his teaching as he worked. He would fire questions at the poor students and woe betide anyone who couldn't answer him. He would pick on them again and again, trying to make them look as foolish as he could. Many a student would leave the lecture with tears in their eyes.

It was in this theatre that I had a nasty accident. Because it was such an old building, there was the remains of a fireplace, and the mantlepiece was still there. On this mantlepiece was a line of kidney dishes with various substances in them, and such things as scalpels, needles for injections, in fact anything sharp. These had to be sterilized with some kind of formula as you couldn't boil or steam sharp instruments. I had been changing the liquids in these kidney dishes and I was pouring Lysol into one of them when the Lysol splashed and went straight into my eye. Lysol is benzalkonium chloride, but it has hydrogen peroxide in it and it burns. I raced to the sink and stuck my head under the running water to wash it out, but after a while Sister thought I'd done enough and I should get on with the work. My eye was so sore and when I came off duty, I went to the sick nurses' bay to see if I could get something to help. I wasn't seeing very well. They immediately sent me to the Ophthalmic specialist that was on duty. He examined my eye and was furious.

"Why didn't you come to me immediately?" he asked.

I didn't have an answer except that I was working and I was told to stay there.

"Well," he said. "You'll be lucky if I can save the sight in your eye."

This frightened the life out of me. It was arranged for me to be taken up to Light Sick Nurses. I had both eyes bandaged and I had to stay that way for the next two weeks. This meant that I had to have everything done for me as I couldn't see at all. It was hard. People would come and go and I would have no idea who they were. At the end of my stay there, I had the bandages removed. The nurse removing them said, "Oh, what beautiful eyes you've got, I had no idea." So that pepped me up a bit. The other time that I landed in Light Sick Nurses was when they thought I had hepatitis and I was there long enough to make a small boob-tube by hand for myself. So the time wasn't wasted.

ONE OF THE wards I enjoyed the most was Grey Ward. It was a men's orthopaedic. This meant that almost all the patients were men who had broken limbs, and were not really ill, only incapacitated. Still, there were a few memorable cases.

There was a young man who'd broken his neck. This meant he was quadriplegic, unable to move any part of his body. He was on a special kind of bed, only a little bigger than his body—it didn't need to be any bigger because he couldn't move, but it made it easier for us to deal with his care. He had a kind of stirrup shaped piece screwed into his head just above the ears. It was attached to the bed and exerted a stable but constant pull on his neck. He had to be turned over every four hours and that included massage of all pressure points. To turn him over there was a replica of the bed placed on top of him, it was open at the top so that it supported his head but he could lie face down, and then he was firmly strapped around both beds, which were then swivelled over. So, the young man was turned, and the top bed removed.

There was a very young boy in the ward who technically should have been in the Children's Hospital, but because he had some kind of rare disease he was in this men's ward. The disease he had made his bones quite chalky, and they could break without any warning and for no reason. The poor kid could not look forward to much of a life, but the men in the ward treated him well.

The Red Cross and other organisations used to come around with their traymobiles full of various thing to make the patients' stay in hospital be a bit more pleasant. One lot used to bring the necessary material and set the men to work making stuffed toys. Most of the men didn't need any stuffed toys but it was something to do. Once they'd given these toys to any children in their lives, we nurses were the lucky ones who had leftover toys given to us. One of the favourite toys was Donald Duck dressed in our favourite football colours (Go Sturt!) I was also given a little rabbit, a white lamb, a kangaroo, a scottie dog and a koala. I remember the man who gave me the koala was called Mr Luck. I named the koala Lucky. I used these toys to decorate the nursery when my children came along.

There was a man in the ward who had been a pearl diver and had got the Bends. He was in a wheelchair and was almost a permanent resident. His name was Ali ben Sulla and he came from New Guinea. He'd been in the Australian Army and was a paratrooper during the war, and because he was originally from New Guinea he and others of his troop had been dropped in to infiltrate the enemy camp. He didn't talk much about it, but when it came to Anzac Day he was so sad that he couldn't be at the dawn service. He was allowed to go out if anyone could take him, but his wife left him when he became paralysed, and he had no other family in Australia. When I found out that he wished to go to the dawn service, as I had a late shift that day, another girl and I decided to take him. We got up early and off we went, pushing his wheelchair along North Terrace in the early hours of the morning. He was so grateful and it did us good to have the walk too. After that we would take Ali out to the pictures or other places he wanted to go. I understand he eventually was sent out to

Bedford Park where he could get some employment and be looked after.

Besides my little sojourn to Magill, we also had to do a stint in Hampstead at the Northfield Infectious Diseases Ward. Once again, off I went on my own, and this time I found myself in the polio ward. There were very few patients in this ward but they required a lot of hard work as they were paralysed. They had to have every little thing done for them. We had one man who was in an iron lung. That was an interesting case, although the work was very mundane, basically doing the same thing over and over for the poor man. When he wanted to read, we put a glass frame on the front of the iron lung and lay the paper or book on the frame so he could read it from his lying down position. The only problem was the nurses had to turn every page for him, which demonstrates how tedious the nursing was.

There was a young fellow, Richard, who had been able to come out of the iron lung. He had made a little progress and could move his fingers but not his arms. He lay in bed planning ways to exercise his body to make it work again. He had some balloons beside the bed and several times a day he would get the balloons and blow into them, trying to get them to inflate. He didn't have the strength in his chest to get them to stretch, but he never gave up. Another favourite game of his was when we had to do his four-hourly back care. We would roll him over on his side, wash all the pressure points, dry them and then massage them with methylated spirits. In those days we were all wearing suspenders to keep our stockings up and while we were doing the pressure points for him, he would get his hands over to our legs and try to get hold of a suspender and ping it. Although he was certain he would work out ways to exercise himself and improve, he was told by all the doctors that he was as good as he would ever get. However, Richard never gave up. He and one of the trained staff fell in love and he was determined he would get better and one day put his arms around her. It was some years later that I learned he had persevered and got out of hospital and into a wheelchair. Eventually he was able to lift his arms to put around his wife. He led a full life and went on to be a disability advocate in the political world.

While at Hampstead, I spent most of my time in the polio ward, but I did have one night in the whooping cough ward with all those poor little mites gasping for breath. It was horrible. Then I was sent to a ward to care for people with other diseases. The most interesting one was a man who'd been brought in from a foreign ship. I don't know what nationality he was, but he had leprosy. All nursing staff were required to go and see him and observe, because it was such a little-known disease in Australia. He was a very nice man and didn't seem to mind being quizzed and treated like a curiosity. I guess it had all been explained to him beforehand and his permission sought. Really the only thing that was visible about his complaint was the skin seemed to be thick and reminded me of an elephant's skin.

In the grounds of the Northfield Wards at Hampstead, there was a section which was just geriatrics. It was staffed with girls who were not trained. They seemed to be carers rather than training nurses like us. I don't know where they fitted into things. They seemed to be looking after the elderly residents of this establishment and didn't have the same rules as us. We referred to them as blue nurses as they wore a blue uniform and a small veil tied behind the head. We training nurses wore pink check uniform with white apron and silly little peak cap on top. We were never allowed to wear our uniform out in the public. We had to travel out to Northfield on the bus and, as it got very crowded, we often had to stand all the way. You can imagine our frustration when one day, after a hard day's work, we were coming home on the bus, standing as usual, when a couple of blue nurses got on wearing their uniforms. Immediately a kind gentleman stood up and gave them his seat, saying, "you should always stand up for a nurse, they work so hard." We were not impressed.

Another area we had to have experience in was back at the RAH, in either the Lomman or Lundie Wards. These were always referred to as 'the new wards', even though by the time I got there, they were a long way from new. There was little that I had to do with Lundie but I was always aware of it because that was the surgical ward Margaret was in after her operation. On one occasion when I was working in casualty, I was taking a patient up to the ward and I had all the relatives in the lift with me. When the lift door opened at Lundie Ward, I pushed the barouche through and there was a nurse standing at the door waiting. When she saw us she said with a voice of horror, "not another one!" It had been take day in Lundie, which meant any surgical cases would have been sent to the surgical wards. Take days were always madness as you never knew what cases would be coming in, nor how many. This nurse who had been waiting by the lift was probably thinking, "Oh no, not more work." So I said to her, "It's okay, it's not for you." That was very much the wrong thing to say. The son of the patient just flew at me.

"My Mother is not an 'it'!" he said, and he took me to task properly. Of course I was mortified, and determined to be careful in future to refer to each one as a person, not a case.

I did the usual six weeks at Lomman, and I enjoyed myself while there. The most interesting part of it was an old Aboriginal man who was a patient there. He was very old, grey haired, but strangely he had blue eyes. He came from a tribe somewhere beyond Oodnadatta and he knew nothing of white European ways. When I came to the ward he was already there and everyone was struggling with him as he could not speak a word of English, and so we had to guess a lot. The other men around him did their best to help us by keeping an eye out and letting us know how he was going. His name was Labby Pepper, and the poor old man must have thought everyone was out to get him. He'd to have his foot amputated and so that was strange for him. He was given hospital gowns to wear but, as he was used to having nothing on, he left the gown flowing open at all times, exposing everything. When we gave him his meals he never used the cutlery but just ate it with his hands. He always hid the knife from his meals—we would search his bed to find it. On one occasion, a young Aboriginal social worker was asked to visit him, hoping he could help the hospital understand more about him. The social worker told us the reason he kept hiding the knives was that he intended to find the people who had taken his foot, and kill them. Then one day the doctor came in and said someone was needed to take Labby Pepper down to the photography department to have the stump of his leg photographed. I was the nurse on duty in his corner, so it fell to me. When they put him on the barouche the poor old man struggled to get away. I took his hands and he clung to me, talking in his own language all the time. My guess is that the last time they took him out of the ward like this he came back without a foot. Anyway we had the photos done and we took him back. This time he talked all the way happily, still clinging onto my hand. From then on he always got animated when I came near his bed. It seemed he felt sure I'd saved his other foot, but the other men all teased me and said: "You want to watch out nurse, you don't know what he is saying." Finally, the physiotherapist came and fitted him for crutches and tried to teach him how to use them. He did his best but the doctor was sure that as soon as he got away from us he would use the stump of his leg and it would get just as thick and leathery as his other foot. The last thing I remember about Labby Pepper was taking him out onto the balcony to sit in the sunshine. Once again he became very animated and talked and talked, mentioning Oodnadatta frequently and pointing to the north. He obviously wanted to go home.

My training in Adelaide was rushing to an end and I was being given more and more senior positions. One of the last wards I worked in was Bice Women's Medical and it was a hard ward to work in. Women, on the whole, were not easy to nurse. They seemed to do a lot of grizzling. The ward was quite big and busy and when we came on duty, the visitors were all still there. One patient was a Greek girl and every day her relatives would visit and crowd around her bed. She was only twenty-one and engaged to be married, but she was suffering from total kidney failure. As at that time there was no dialysis, she was slowly dying and in terrible pain. Every night when it came time for the visitors to leave her relatives would come to my desk and plead with me to get the doctor to do something to help her. There was no point in contacting the doctor. He would not have come anyway as he was as helpless as I was, but it was a battle every night to get them to leave.

We found the patients were always demanding attention, even though it was nighttime. The work was constant. As I was the senior nurse it was my job to write the report each night. I would start that at about 3am, recording everything that had taken place during the night. But by that time of night it was hard to keep my eyes open and I often found myself dropping off, then having to go over and correct the report. On one occasion we had a lady in a bed about two-thirds of the way up the ward, and she would constantly call out during the night.

"Pan Nurse, I want a pan!" she would yell on top note. Then when the nurse took the pan to her she wouldn't do anything.

On this particular night I was very weary and while writing the report I was aware of this lady yelling "Pan, I want a pan." As I was writing I must have dropped off to sleep. When I woke I found I'd written in the report: *Reasonably quiet night. Mrs ... a bit noise but pan given by her friends ...* and the writing tapered off in a squiggly line. I sure had some touching up to do there.

CASUALTY WAS one of my favourite places to work and I had plenty of experience there. In 1954 the Government had built a new hospital called the Queen Elizabeth Maternity Hospital at Woodville, but over the years they decided that it should be extended to a general hospital. In 1959 the work on that project was completed and the New Queen Elizabeth Hospital was opened. This needed a lot of extra staff and of course it had to be trained staff to get it off the ground. The answer to this problem was to take a selection of senior staff from the RAH for six weeks, to get things started. What happened then at the RAH, was that instead of the usual rotations, some of the senior staff were kept in their current wards for an extra six weeks. As I was now a senior nurse I was selected to work in casualty. I'd just spent the last six weeks here already, but it was good experience and became handy in later years when I joined the St John's Ambulance.

Casualty was always a very busy place and because it was the up-front area, you never knew what cases would be coming in. We often had men come in during the working day, and very often it was to have small bits of steel removed from their eye because they were grinding or cutting steel with no eye protection. It never failed to amaze me how very hard the surface of the eye is. I usually had to help the surgeon remove the foreign object that would be embedded firmly in the eye. It had to be flicked out with a pointed instrument.

Saturday nights were frantic as Rolly Park Motor Racing was always held then, and we would have case after case come in from that. Then there were all the patients who were brought in for various reasons by ambulance. After they were dealt with, we had to take them to the various "take" wards to be admitted. I think the most challenging thing I had to deal with was when a European man came in, holding a great ball of newspaper to his mouth. It appeared that he'd had his lip bitten off. We got him onto the table and cleaned it all up, and I asked him how it had happened, was it a dog or something that had bitten him?

"No," he said. "It was my friend!"

Wow. With friends like that who needs enemies? We got him cleaned up and sent him off to theatre. The next thing I knew, there was a nurse looking for me and asking where the man's lip was, as I hadn't sent it up. I told her I hadn't seen his lip.

"He said he gave it to you wrapped in newspaper."

Oh dear. What a conundrum. I raced out to find the paper but to no avail, the bins had been emptied and it was gone. There was nothing I could do. Fortunately, we didn't have to deal with patients once they left casualty, so I never found out what they did for the poor man.

On one occasion, there was a commotion in the Eleanor Harrald Nurses Home. I had settled down in bed. It wasn't late but I went to bed early as a rule. I was just dozing off when I heard much loud talking and walking around in the passage outside my room. When I opened the door I found quite a group of people in the passage, mostly police officers and some sisters. When I asked what was going on I found one of the girls had seen an intruder in the home, who then seemed to disappear. Hence the police call out. Police officers seemed to be everywhere and a couple of the nurses, and me, spent the time hanging out of the window at the end of the passage, watching proceedings. After some time they realised that the person was one of the nurse's boyfriends who had wanted to get in touch with her, and had gone to the window of her room—only it wasn't her room, and the nurse whose room it *was* screamed and yelled that there was a prowler. Of course the poor fellow ran for his life as the police came and spread throughout the nurses' home. When all was said and done, the police were lined up ready to be sent back to work only to find there were two missing. That caused a bit of a ruckus but it was soon sorted, and off they went, leaving everything nice and quiet again.

The very last ward I had to work in was Victoria Ward. This was another of the Floor Wards and it had a terrible reputation because of Charge Sister Tericky. In her training days, she had topped the class in everything and was awarded a gold medal for excellence, but she was the absolute epitome of a person having been taught in theory but not in practise. Because of her supposed skills, she was one of the few charge sisters who did not have a staff nurse in the ward. She only had senior nurses who were considered the best nurses, to replace the staff nurse. So here I was, my last ward, and senior nurse.

This sister was the most disorganised person I've ever known. In every other ward the system was clear—you knew what to do, your role was clear, and everything went smoothly. But in this ward, you would only just be getting on with your work when the sister would come and tell you to do something else. This often interfered with someone else who'd been sent to do a task that wasn't their job. It was frustrating that no one could get their work done and everyone ended up having to work overtime. You didn't get paid for overtime in those days but were expected to do your work within the hours allocated. Things were always a mess when the sister was there. On the other hand, when she had her day off, I was in charge, and I saw to it that everyone attended to their own work. We never worked overtime on those days.

One day, because of the sister's bumbling around, I overdosed one of the patients. The doctor had been to see this man and was watching him carefully. He noted that the patient had not had his injection. He instructed me to give it to him immediately, which I did. At the time, Sister was out of the room having her morning lunch. When she came back she casually said that she must chart the injection that she'd given this man earlier. What a hoo-hah when I told her that doctor had ordered the injection and I'd done it. I was worried about it, but as she was back in the ward, now it was her responsibility, so she was the one who had to report it and sort it out.

It was in this ward where I had my worst encounter with the Italian community. We had a lot of Italian women working as domestics at the hospital. They were all very nice people, but they used to warn me to have nothing to do with 'that lot' who came from the south of Italy. Apparently, they were 'a bad lot'. All this happened, and I didn't know that one day my daughter would marry a man from the south of Italy.

But at the time, I had a patient who fulfilled all the warnings—a young man in his early twenties who sat up in bed and demanded attention at all times. On one occasion he called to me as I was racing past his bed and ordered me to get him something immediately. I asked if he could wait a moment as I was attending to another patient, but he screamed at me to get what he wanted. He eventually threatened to kill me with a knife if I didn't do as he said. I had to draw myself up to my full height and, in my best sergeant major voice, told him to be quiet or he would get nothing. It must have worked as he didn't give me any trouble from then on, but I got plenty of dark looks.

When I was leaving Victoria Ward, I was left with wounds on my arms. We had an old gentleman who was suffering from dementia and he had the devil in him, and no doubt about that. He seemed to have super strength, and when he decided he would do something he was impossible to handle. Because of this he had to be strapped into his bed for safety's sake. The last day I was there, this man decided to go wandering. We had to get him back into bed. He fought us all the way and it took five of us, including the doctor, to get him onto the bed. While I was holding him down, he got his hand around my arm and dug his fingernails into my flesh, digging little pieces out of my arm. Mind you, his fingernails were cut back as far as they could go. So a row of little sores on my arm was my goodbye gift from the Royal Adelaide Hospital.

11

JIM ENTERS THE SCENE

Throughout my story so far, I've referred to my husband, Jim, and the many ways we were connected even before we realised. This is the story of how we finally and properly met.

Our first encounter was the time my father stopped and asked Jim for directions and concluded he was a "bloody idiot." But he wasn't on my radar then.

Our proper meeting was facilitated through a patient I'd nursed at the Booleroo Centre District Hospital. This young woman, Yvonne Launer, had needed surgery on her feet, which meant she had to stay in hospital for a long period. During this time, I got to know her well. While Yvonne was recovering, she told me about her fiancé, Don, and their wedding plans. When she was discharged, she invited me over to her parents' place and we spent quite a lot of time together and remained friends even when I started training at the Royal Adelaide Hospital. Eventually Yvonne asked if I would be one of her bridesmaids. I had already gotten to know her family well, but I hadn't met her fiancé's brother,

Jim. I knew he was a farmer from Melrose, but I only knew what Yvonne had told me.

I spent a lot of time together with Yvonne preparing for the wedding day. She was an excellent dressmaker, and she made our dresses—a dark pink chiffon with a collar that stood out and rolled like the petals of a rose.

And then the beautiful day arrived. Jim was best man, and he took my arm to be my escort for the day. I must say his wedding speech didn't make him seem very romantic. Jim teased his brother about having been caught, and then he stated, with conviction, that he would not be caught the same way. He also left me at the wedding to find my own way home, while he went on to a Rural Youth rally. I had to be dropped home by Yvonne's brother. So that was that—or so I thought.

Not long after, I was home in Wilmington on one of the rare occasions I got time off from the RAH. I was resting after a long stint of night duty and while sound asleep, Mum woke me to say there was someone on the phone for me.

It was Jim.

"Yeah, g'day," he said. "I wonder if you want to go with me to a housewarming for Yvonne and Don?"

"I might," came my sleepy reply. "Or I might not. We're shearing, so I'll see."

"Oh. Alright," Jim answered, and we both hung up.

"Who was that?" Mum asked me. It was only then I woke up properly and was horrified to realise how rude and disinterested I had sounded. I took Mum's advice and called him straight back. He accepted my apology and excuse of only being half awake.

And so, we went on our first date together—the housewarming. As usual it was quite a rowdy affair when all the young people gathered. Even though it was a date, I took my duty as bridesmaid very seriously—even beyond the wedding—so I followed Yvonne to help with all the organising and hosting. Unfortunately, it was a wet winter's day and everything around the house was soaked and muddy. I answered the door to one guest, and when he entered he went straight to Yvonne's nice new white mats in front of the fireplace and wiped his muddy shoes on them. I grabbed the mats and threw them in the bedroom, hoping to protect them from more abuse. It was no good. They couldn't be recovered. He had ruined the lot with red sticky mud.

When the evening came to an end, Jim ended our first date with an invitation for a second. He asked if I'd like to go with him to a Rural Youth bus tour reunion.

The Rural Youth was a state organisation that had branches in many rural towns, including Melrose. It focused on teaching youth practical and useful things in life, but also giving them fun social activities. I'd not had anything to do with them to this point, but Jim was actively involved. They organised guest speakers, dances, debates and public speaking competitions, and social events with other clubs. Being a rural organisation, they also had competitions for things like cattle and sheep judging, hay bale stacking and tractor driving.

Jim used to get up to all sorts of mischief with the Rural Youth. Once, at a fancy dress dance, he went dressed as the old television character, Ma Kettle. During one of the activities, someone dressed as a gorilla approached him and asked, as he was a lady gorilla, would Jim—being a lady—accompany him to the ladies' toilet? They entered the room for a fleeting moment, and all the occupants screamed, so they ran out as quickly as possible. This was the kind of nonsense they went on with (and I might add, the gorilla was one of the advisors from Adelaide).

The Rural Youth bus tour reunion—our second date—was a dinner-dance held at the Freemasons Hall on North Terrace in Adelaide. Since I needed to get back to work at the Royal Adelaide Hospital, I saw the opportunity of catching a free ride back to the city, if nothing else. After the dance, Jim, quite cool and calm, asked me if I'd like to take a drive up to Windy Point to take photos of the city lights.

Really, I thought to myself. *How dumb does this fellow think I am?* Windy point was a popular place for young couples to park, and I knew that. Nonetheless, I agreed to go—and I made him get out of the car to take photos when we got there.

But Jim wasn't put off. In fact, within *three* weeks, he proposed to me. And I said *yes!*

The proposal went like this: I was home from the RAH for a weekend, visiting Jim at his parents' property, Gumville, Melrose. We were sitting together on the lounge-room floor by the fire, eating oranges. Suddenly, out of nowhere, Jim said, "Jennette Hamlyn, will you marry me?"

I'm not sure what made him so confident to ask me in that moment. Neither is he, truth be told. When people asked why he popped the question so quickly, he's told them: "Nothing was further from my mind at the time. The Lord just got hold of my tongue and flapped it up and down." There is, another version he tells: "I had to catch her before she got away."

I think Jim was a bit surprised when I answered a decisive "Yes!" He told me that he then worried for weeks, wondering what on earth the two of us were going to talk about once we were married.

My problem was different—I had to go and tell my current boyfriend, Bob, the peanut king, that I was engaged. All that was left to do was convince Dad that Jim was not the bloody idiot he'd first judged, but rather, a generous, good-natured, hardworking, prosperous farmer—and a good catch by any father's standard. Eventually, it was Dad's boss, Mr Maynard Mould, who gave his endorsement after meeting Jim for the first time. "He's a good bloke. Jennette should hang her hat up to him."

And so, we were engaged to be married. While the proposal only took three weeks, preparing for the wedding took a bit longer. The courtship began with me still working in Adelaide and Jim working on the farm at Melrose. He'd bought himself a little Volkswagen which he drove down to Adelaide on most weekends when I wasn't working. He'd arrive in the middle of the day and pick me up at the Eleanor Harrald Nurses Home. We'd find a suitable place to park, sometimes on the lawns of the Torrens or even back at Windy Point. Occasionally we'd drive down to Auntie Ollie's at Woodville, or visit Jim's Auntie Alice, who also lived locally. But we were always back at the nurses' home on Saturday, in time for Jim to drop me off and get on the road back home, so he was there for church on Sunday morning.

There were a few times that I was able to get up north and visit Jim on the farm, but we only ever had one day a week off, so it was rare. If I had night duty we were given more time. After a night duty shift I had the day when I was supposed to be sleeping, then the next day (Saturday, my day off for that week, then Sunday, (my day off for the next week), and Monday I started work at 11am for a late shift. This gave me a long weekend of sorts. Later in our courtship Jim paid for me to fly to Port Pirie on a couple of occasions, but that didn't go down well with Jim's father, who wasn't pleased he was spending so much money. But we managed our courtship well and because I was so far away, we didn't have any interference from anyone else.

While working in the hospital we weren't allowed to wear any jewellery on duty, so my sparkling new engagement ring had to come off every time I was on duty. Dad got busy and made me a tiny, leather, ring case with a safety pin on the back. I'd keep my ring in it and pin the case in the top pocket of my uniform. I had an awful shock one night when I was hurrying to get on duty. I'd taken my ring off but in my rush to put it in the little case I dropped it. I was in the old lift in Bice building. It was one of those lifts that had a concertina door enclosing the lift, and another outer one at each floor. There was a big gap in between that fell right down the shaft. My ring dropped while I was in the lift, then bounced across the floor towards the first concertina door. I imagined the horror of never seeing my ring again. Thankfully, it hit one of the metal pieces on the concertina and bounced back and I was able to retrieve it. I couldn't believe my luck and I never took the ring off in a lift again.

Before I'd met Jim, my plan had been to finish my certification to become a general nurse, get specialist training in midwifery, and eventually join the Flying Doctors. But once I became engaged, my plans had to change. Women couldn't remain in the profession once married. I still intended to get through my general nurse training though, and I calculated it would be wrapped up about a month before our wedding. However, it never happened. At the time, after you passed each training stage, you had to sign in for the next class—it was not automatic. The only trouble was if you didn't sign up in time you missed out until the next exam. Such was my bad luck. For some time I'd been trying to get into the invalid cookery class, but every time I tried they said I was too late and I'd have to try again. This kept happening, and soon my final exam came along, and I still hadn't done invalid cookery. I did my finals but could not be passed because of this missing class. They said I could do my finals again at a later date when I'd completed the course. I weighed everything up and decided, considering I was not allowed to nurse after I was married, I'd just drop the lot.

When I finished at the RAH, I did not have to look for another nursing job as I was getting married in six weeks. But just to build up the coffers I enquired with Matron Catford to see if there was anything going at the Booleroo Hospital. She was pleased to offer me some night duty.

"How much night duty?" I asked.

"As much as you can do," she replied. So I agreed to do four weeks straight with one night a week off. She showed me over the newly constructed areas. The old jail had been removed, and now had a very nice Midwifery section—two private bedrooms and one double room, the delivery room and the nursery at the end of the passage. When she showed me the nursery I said to her, "Only five cribs, is that enough?"

"Oh yes, we never have more than two or three babies at a time."

Everything was lovely and new. On the other side of the passage was a door leading out to the back of the hospital, where there were new showers for the Midwifery patients. This adjoined the old sterilizing room, and a new area for outpatients and administration. I started my night duty straight away and, after the gruelling pace of the RAH, I looked forward to an easy time in the lead up to our wedding. Well, I got that wrong, didn't I? It seemed that all the expectant mothers thought this was a good time to have their babies, and in they came. One, two, three, four, five. Then number six, and the night nurse said to me, "where are you going to put this baby?"

I rose to the occasion. "We'll use the crib from the Mid room, surely there won't be any more now."

But once again I was wrong. In came number seven. Horror of horrors, what do I do now in the early hours of the morning? Not to be beaten I went to the cupboard in the sterilizing room and took the bottom draw out of the cupboard, emptied it and made it up as a crib. That being done, I decided I'd done my duty as a nurse. Now I was to enter the realm of matrimony, become a wife and eventually a mother.

Yvonne and Don's wedding, where Jim and I were partners 1958

12

THE BIG DAY ARRIVES

Having finished my time at the Booleroo hospital, the next thing was to get down to Adelaide. We'd decided to have the wedding in the city because all our aunties, uncles and extended family lived there. We got married at the Flinders Street Baptist Church, which is where my grandparents were married. It was an exciting time as both our families were getting ready for the day. We stayed at Auntie Ollie's place, which was natural as I'd been living there while I was at the RAH. Jim and his family stayed with relatives too, some at Auntie Alice and Uncle Maurice's, and others at Auntie Lou Marner's.

Everything was going well, all organised for the next day. I was even able to rest a little, until I got a telephone call. It came from one of the girls I'd worked with at the RAH. She was from Laura, a town near Wilmington, and we'd become quite friendly over the years. She was an excellent pianist and vocalist and had agreed to sing and play the piano and organ for the wedding. Imagine my horror when I received a message to say she'd decided she wasn't going to come to the wedding.

"What? But she's responsible for all the music!" I cried. What was I going to do now? Thank the Lord for Uncle Wal. Uncle Wal was a man who owned a large steel construction business, and he used to put on Christmas parties and other occasions for his workmen. He had a lady he specifically employed for the purpose of doing the music at such events. She was the very one I needed. Uncle Wal got on the phone and after a bit of arranging, I had my music for the church, but I had to cancel any ideas of singing or dancing at the reception. I wasn't too worried as we were a family who had fun, and it didn't matter if they couldn't do one thing, they would just enjoy themselves some other way.

Dad's boss invited us to have dinner on the night before the wedding. We met him at the Ambassador's Hotel in King William Street and he shouted us to a scrumptious meal. He asked me what I would like to drink at the meal and jokingly I said, "Nothing but champagne." And with that, he ordered champagne all round. I think that was the first time I'd ever tasted it. But I liked it.

Auntie Ollie's gardener was so thrilled that I was going to have the wedding at the house that he specially cleaned up, tying up everything, even the roses—and the ties were quite clearly seen in all the photos. My sister Margaret, soon to be sister-in-law Yvonne and cousin, Raelene were my bridesmaids, and my sister-in-law, Von arrived with my nieces, Vicki and Pauline, who were the flower girls. The photographer came and took photos in the lounge, the dining room and bedroom, then outside on the lawn with the archway of roses neatly tied up, in the sunken garden, and along the drive at the side of the house. I mention about where the photos were taken because twenty-three years later it would be repeated when my daughter, Meredith, was married from the same house.

Time was drawing near and soon I heard Uncle Wal call out.

"The cars are here." he said. "They don't look like much."

It had been Jim's job to order the cars for the wedding and he'd chosen to contact a friend who had a business in this area. Jim never heard back from the man, so he contacted another firm to do the job. The next thing I knew, Uncle Wal was standing there telling me there were two lots of cars out the front. And he wanted to know what I was going to do about it. Dressed in my wedding gown with all the trimmings I headed for the front yard to try and sort out the mess, but just as I got to the door Uncle Wal came in and said, "It's alright, the driver of the second lot of cars told the first lot to get lost." And they did, never to be heard of again. And the second lot of cars were much nicer. I had the luxury of three big black Fords done up with ribbons on the front, drivers in full chauffer uniform, white gloves and all.

At last it was off to the wedding. We got into the car and Dad told me he had made a terrible mistake. He'd sent his best suit to the dry-cleaners and when it came back he just packed it to come to Adelaide. It wasn't until he took it out to get dressed he realised it was the wrong one. It was his old suit which he'd bought when he got out of the army about twelve years before. It had to do as we didn't have another one for him to change into. Thankfully he was still the same size.

The wedding went well. It was a very wet day which made all the farmers smile—we had been in drought up until then. Jim's father, Dick Bishop, had said to me, "I've always said if a man can keep a wife when there's a drought, he will be okay always." This drought broke on our wedding day. It rained most of the day, there was snow on Mount Remarkable that morning, and every time I went outside the sun came out and shone. What more could you want?

At our reception there were various speeches, and then Uncle Wal proposed a toast to us as the new couple.

"I used to find it very difficult," he started off, "because I never knew who was going to Bob in and who was going to Bob out." Ha ha.

Of course there were no Bobs in the picture on this day.

We had a few photos taken including cutting the cake—we pretended for the photos, the actual cake cutting wasn't done until later. Then the photographer was off and we didn't see him again. When we finally got the photos back, there was a mystery. Nearly every photo taken of the guests outside the church showed a young man right up front. Neither Jim nor I have any idea who he was to this day.

THE HONEYMOON

With the wedding safely performed we set out on the honeymoon. Our first stop was The Ambassadors Hotel in King William Street. We woke the next morning at 6am—a strange hour for honeymooners. Jim rifled through his bag and discovered he'd forgotten to bring a razor. Perhaps he thought that was what he got married for—so a wife could pack his bags for him. It was imperative that he shave as no new bride will tolerate a sandpaper face. Luckily, I remembered that Dad's boss, was staying in the same hotel. But we had to be at the airport early, so poor Mr Mould got a very early call from an embarrassed bridegroom to see if he could lend him his electric shaver.

Shaving delays notwithstanding, we made the flight to Melbourne on time. We arrived in that cold, dismal city and booked in at the Victoria Hotel. As we were going up to our room the elevator stopped at another floor for other people. It could only be Jim who would recognise somebody in a faraway, strange city. As the elevator door was closing, he said "I know that man out there, I think."

"Shush! It doesn't matter!" I told him, and pulled him back before he exited to chase down his acquaintance. This was our honeymoon after all.

He stayed put and seemed to forget the incident until there was a knock on the door.

"Surprise!"

Wouldn't you know it. A group of young people from the South Australian Rural Youth were in Melbourne on a bus tour and couldn't resist asking their old buddy and his new wife to join them for the evening. Jim couldn't resist accepting, this being part of his social personality that I was beginning to know. I made it clear that we should not spend too long at the party—being the shy one.

Unlike modern facilities, the Victoria Hotel had a common bathroom and toilet shared by a number of rooms. Whether Jim had ever been to such an establishment before or not, I do not know, but he didn't seem concerned about having to go down the hallway, from the room to the bathroom, without a bathrobe. He'd seen the way his parents had solved such a problem. His father often borrowed his mother's heavy, woollen, checkered, men's dressing-gown, to dash to the outhouse. He hadn't packed a dressing gown, as he figured he would borrow mine.

Unfortunately, he wasn't expecting what I'd packed.

"Certainly, you may borrow my dressing gown," I told him, holding up my delicate, lace-trimmed negligee. "Be my guest."

The following morning, we boarded the boat that travelled between Melbourne and Burnie, Tasmania. As it turned out, our trip was on the last boat to make the crossing before the new Princess of Tasmania came into service. Even though we weren't sailing on the new sea vessel across the Bass Strait it was still a new and exciting experience for a couple of inland dwellers. We wanted to make the most of every onboard service available, so sat in the spacious lounge to enjoy the company and conversation of the other passengers. This old boat had no stabilisers fitted but everything was beautiful as we glided out of the calm waters of Port Phillip Bay—until we hit the rip at the mouth of the bay opening onto the open sea. I thought the whole thing was going to roll over backwards. With the boat pitching and tossing, I began to feel decidedly green. I pleaded urgently with Jim to cease all conversations and head back to the cabin. Part way there I instinctively knew I wouldn't make it. I alerted Jim and he hurried ahead to find a ladies' toilet. Once he located one, he returned and ushered me, without a second thought, straight inside. Once again, Jim was in the ladies' room. This time he didn't realise his trespass, overcome with concern. Later, we were able to laugh and thank the Lord there were no other ladies around.

Tasmania loomed as an island of reprieve—terra firma—and at one point, I thought of staying there the rest of our lives in preference to undergoing the torturous sea-sickness again. Jim hired a station sedan big enough to carry the camping gear that we also hired. Soon the horrible nighttime crossing faded from our memories. We set off on our tour of the Apple Isle.

We started off with a good look around Launceston. The hydro-electric scheme they had going was mind blowing to us—we couldn't believe how much water was gushing out. After our sojourn there we set off for our wandering tour of the island. I spotted the name 'Melrose' on the map and it wasn't far from Launceston, so we decided to head there. It was well named. A small town about the same size as our Melrose. There wasn't a lot to see, so after having a bite of lunch we headed south along the middle highway, observing farmland very like our own. As evening approached, we intended to find a place to park for the night. Although we'd been travelling for a long time, there hadn't even been enough room on the side of the road to pull right off. I suggested to Jim we turn down one of the side roads. I'd seen a man on a horse across the paddock, and thought perhaps we could get some information as to where we should park.

We drove up to the man, told him our problem, and he very kindly waved us up to some trees on the side of the paddock. "You can camp over there if you like. Just come up to the house if you need anything—milk, butter, eggs or anything like that."

We thanked him and made our way up to the campsite where we unpacked the gear that had been given us with the car. Our station sedan was a new innovation of the time and we felt very privileged to have something so modern. There were two big trunks in the back. One of them had a small primus stove and everything we might need to make our meals, and the other held a rolled-up mattress that fitted into the back of the Station Sedan, plus pillows and bedding. The only problem was that because the car was so new, they hadn't yet put curtains on the windows, so once we went to bed, we were able to be seen by the whole world.

The next morning, after we were up and packed, we went down to the house to thank the farmer, Mr Gregg, and his wife for their hospitality. They seemed quite amused to have hosted new honeymooners who'd never been to Tasmania before. We exchanged details before we left.

Off we went again, heading south with the idea of staying at a place called Holiday Lodge. We drove at our leisure and stopping whenever we wanted to look at the surroundings. I was particularly interested in the wattle—it was quite different to our South Australian wattle. Instead of being little round balls of yellow, these flowers were long, thin, creamy-coloured fluff. The growth on the sides of the road was like a rainforest, quite different to our area full of eucalyptus gums. As we approached the Holiday Lodge, we found it hard to tell how to get from the road to the hotel. We stopped to ask a road-worker who gave us good directions—turn left here, and go right there, etc. We said thanks and as we drove off, I said to Jim, "I thought it was on the other side of the road, by the map." Then Jim noticed in the rear vision mirror the man waving his arms frantically and pointing to the opposite side from his directions. Well, we got to Holiday Lodge, and it was a beautiful place. Our rooms looked out over a big golf course surrounded by a rainforest-type scrub. Everything inside was so cosy. There was an older couple there and Jim asked how long they had been staying.

"We came here for a week's holiday, but we're still here five years later," the gentleman said.

We stayed at Holiday Lodge for a couple of days and then set out for Hobart. My Auntie Doss and Uncle Alf and their twin daughters lived in Lindisfarne, on the Southern side of the Derwent River in Hobart. We were invited to stay with them for a few days. We found their home by evening and although we were staying with them, we still camped in their yard—a big area with a lot of growth around it. We weren't completely protected though. In the early hours of the morning, the milkman came to deliver the milk and peered in the windows. He soon hurried off in the other direction.

We had the great fortune to drive to the top of the famous

Mount Wellington, where we experienced snow for the first time in our lives. But, while the snow was a great experience, the outhouse was not. Nature called (as nature often does in out-of-the-way places). Like all good tourist destinations, Mount Wellington had the necessary facilities—that is to say, it had a little, iron-housed long drop-pit, with the door half off its hinges.

"Go ahead. You go first."

"Thank you. No. I'd be happy for you to warm the seat before me."

We still have the photographs of the toilet seat, encrusted with eighteen inches of icy snow. Our trip to the bottom of the mountain was made with great haste.

The next place of interest was a visit to Port Arthur. We took the day and drove down to take in the history of the place. It was a very interesting set-up although there were parts we weren't allowed to go into because they were unsafe. There was a quaint chapel which we were told was never consecrated because there had been a murder in the church. The prison cells were quite creepy. I imagined the poor souls locked in these cells designed for punishment—totally dark, totally silent, no communication with the outside world. It was said that many of the convicts went mad when locked away like that. There was an island that could be seen from the shore, right in the middle of the bay. It was said that as it was almost pure limestone, if any convicts were hanged or executed, their bodies were taken to the island and buried, thus having their remains disappear over time.

While at Lindisfarne, my cousins, Joan and Betty, took us all around the district to show us the sights before we left to go back up the West Coast to Launceston to catch our plane to go home. But before we left, it began to snow, which meant we couldn't go back up the western highway as we didn't have the chains necessary for travel in those conditions. So we had to return up the same middle road we had come down on. As we were travelling, we decided to contact Mr and Mrs Gregg and see if we could stay there on the way. They were very happy to have us again, and instead of camping, they suggested we come to the house and set up there. We still stayed in our bed in the car, but parked near the house, and spent the day with them, having a lovely time.

During the night it snowed again, and when we woke it looked as if everything was in black and white. We had some fun the next day making a snow man with one of the Gregg children, and being shown over their farm.

While we were there, I confided in Mrs Gregg that I was worried about Jim, as he hadn't had a bowel movement for several days. That's the trouble with being a nurse whose job it is to monitor things like bowel movements.

The news soon spread, and for the rest of our stay, it became a regular conversation topic.

"Any luck yet? Has there been any movement?"

Poor Jim, being so scrutinised. Luckily the situation resolved itself eventually.

When it was time to continue on our way home, we got to Launceston, took the hire-car back, then went and got a hotel room for the night. The only problem here was that Jim picked a hotel where the clientele were mostly workmen from the river scheme. When we went down to dinner, the room was full of men—and me.

The next day we flew back to Melbourne. I wasn't going anywhere near the boat again. Our timing was lucky—the stage play "My Fair Lady" was showing in Melbourne. It was the first time in Australia so we were thrilled to be able to see it. After that nice finish we got the plane back to Adelaide, and home again.

We arrived back to Melrose to begin our new life together. I was now a farmer's wife.

Years later, at our home in Gumville, a car drove up our long farm road. There was a man and woman in the car, with a young adult sitting in the back seat.

The man rolled down the window and said, "We're on our honeymoon and wondered if we could camp on your place tonight."

Taken aback, Jim said, "Well you could go down by the creek if you like."

The man chuckled and said, "You don't know who I am do you?"

"No," Jim replied.

"We're the Greggs from Tasmania."

Jim was amazed and immediately brought them inside. The amazing thing was, when Jim asked me if I knew who they were, I looked at the young man and somehow knew it was young Gregg, all grown up.

It's funny how these connections are made.

19th September 1959. Jim and Jenny Bishop with parents, Art and Alice Hamlyn, and Ella and Dick (Walter) Bishop. Folks started to call me Jenny at this stage in my life.

13

THE FARM IS OURS ... SORT OF

We arrived home from our honeymoon on the Thursday before the Melrose Show. We had planned to have a whole fortnight away but Jim wanted to get home in time for the show and so our holiday was cut short. Why the show was so important, I quite honestly don't know, but it seemed that everyone thought so, and so I joined in.

We spent the first day home getting the selected stud Hereford cattle all washed, dried and ready to present. Then there were flowers to pick and arrange and selections of cookery to transport. We also needed to gather the needlework my mother-in-law, Ella, had been preparing. We got it all to the showgrounds for the judging on show day. The show came and went, with all hands on deck as everyone worked in the various areas of interest, and hopefully had a moment to enjoy the day.

The next day was Sunday, so there was church to attend—our first service as a married couple. We were warmly greeted as newlyweds by the local congregation.

At this point, Jim and I were living at Gumville—the Bishop family farm. My parents-in-law, Ella and Dick, had planned to move from the farmhouse into the home Dick had bought for his mother (now passed), situated opposite the Melrose Primary School. Unfortunately, we got home from our honeymoon and they were still in the farmhouse. Nothing had been done to even prepare for the move. So our first week of married life we had just the front room, which was to be our bedroom.

Don and Yvonne came to help Ella and I pack up the house. Everyone concentrated on getting the older Bishops into their new place, leaving me with Mum and Margaret to clean up after their move, and begin to assemble Jim's and my home. Mum was used to doing this as she had moved so many times in her lifetime. Margaret and I knew the routine too. Mum lamented over the fact that everything was so dirty. She insisted on scrubbing out all the cupboards and places that were not always seen to make sure all was lovely for her daughter to start her married life. Finally, all was cleaned and ready and when Jim came home from his mother's new place, although sparsely furnished, the house looked quite good. Now, the home of Jim's childhood was his own. He was now the boss and master. Though this was yet to be tested.

When Dick and Ella had taken over the Gumville homestead back in the early 1940s, the outside walls were just plain stone, unpainted, with wooden shutters on the windows. When we took up residence in 1959, it had been painted with cream-coloured walls and blue trimmings. Though the porch entrance was at the front, we had to enter at the side of the house, because there was a wire-netting fence around the yard leading to the porch. The front garden area was kept hoed up to keep weeds down. If one tried to enter through the porch door they would have had to push past a 44-gallon drum of kerosine—fuel for the refrigerator.

The house at Gumville was a beautiful, large home with a lot of character. Out the backdoor was a veranda, where once had been an underground water tank. It had been filled in to make an area that Ella used as garden. On the edge of the veranda was Ella's laundry room, complete with a copper, a set of cement wash troughs and a Lightburn 32-volt washing machine. Ella had left the machine for us because in town, you could only use 240 volt. At the back of the laundry was a small stone engine room where we kept the engine and batteries for the 32-volt plant. Behind the engine room was the outside toilet. You really didn't want to go there in the middle of the night. Inside the house, there was a kitchen/family room with a separate room set up as a pantry, but had originally been used as the servants' room. There was a big slow combustion Aga cooker in the fireplace and sink under the kitchen window.

There was a large bathroom with two doors, and from the top passage there was a double door with stained glass windows leading onto a small porch.

We did not have a lot to start with. We had our car, a 1956 Volkswagen, the Mrs Potts irons, the kerosene fridge, and the 32-volt washing machine, and some pieces of furniture. We'd bought a Queen Anne bedroom suite, and I had my camphorwood chest for the bedroom. The bay window in our room was ideal to put a large jardinière with a potted palm. The jardinière was Jim's Grandma Thiselton's wedding gift to us.

We'd also bought a kitchen suite. A table with red laminex and tubular steel chairs with red seats. Other than that, we only had furniture left behind by Ella or the odd thing that Mum could spare. There were two fold-up beds in one spare room, two small armchairs in the lounge, plus an antique traymobile. After a couple of years, when I'd saved up enough to get my own, I returned these to Ella, especially as the traymobile was a valuable piece. However, we kept the hall table in the passage, and Ella gave us the pianola, as it had been so hard to get into the house, no one wanted to take it out again.

For the first year or so we spent our time getting to know each other and establishing the way our home would be run. At this time, the farm and business—JW Bishop & Co—was still being run by Dick. The two boys basically did as their dad told them. But there was a lot of tension, especially around money.

I settled into the role of a farmer's wife quickly, becoming the all-round cook and bottle washer, shepherd, milkmaid, truckie, and whatever else farmer's wives do before they learn better.

I brought a few animals to the property. Dad insisted that Laddie stay with Margaret, but he gave me a big, seventeen-hand horse named Nekker. Nekker was gentle but broken winded, so he frightened people because of the roaring noise his breathing made. Still, he did the job. I was the only one of the Bishop family who could ride, so I did a lot of mustering of both cattle and sheep.

I had brought my sheep dog, Tip, who was well trained by Dad. Dick took a liking to Tip and wanted to have him, but once he took him out and, when the dog didn't do something as Dick considered it should be done, he kicked him hard in the side. The dog took off and came home to me. From then on Tip wouldn't do anything for Dick, so he missed out there.

I also had my own cow, Mrs Murgatroyde. The arrangement was that any house cows, and the produce from them, belonged to the wives. This meant that both Yvonne and I could milk a few cows, sell the cream, plus supply the house with butter, fresh cream and milk. The eggs were also ours, so we packed any spare eggs into special boxes and sent away to sell. The money from the eggs and cream was ours to use on doing things in the house and garden—a chance to make home more comfortable. The only problem with the system came when one of the stud Heredfords produced twins and a calf needed to be looked after. The Hereford cows often couldn't feed two calves at once, and the job to hand feed always fell to me. Yvonne escaped the task as she had more cows than me to have to attend to. That was okay. They were her personal cows and she got all the money from them. I had to rear the stud calves which meant I didn't have the time or the room to have my own cows. And as they were part of the family stud, Jim only got a quarter of the proceeds. I did feel rather hard done by as I paid to rear these calves, but didn't get any money at all.

I recall on one occasion they brought a bull calf in and told me they would eventually slaughter it as it had something wrong with its feet—it stood on tip-toes, and the feet turned under at the first joint. I pleaded they let me try to save it and I fed it on Sunshine powdered milk for several weeks until its little legs strengthened. I had to pay for the milk as Dick didn't approve of me trying to save the little bull, but when it grew big enough to sell, they sold it for £100 which was top price at the time. Jim got a quarter of the sale price while the others took their share, and I got nothing. And so it went on in this manner. I have to admit I began to resent the system.

It all came to a head when the power in the district was upgraded, and Gumville was finally set up to use 240volt. Jim had invested some of his personal money, but when Dick found out, he was insistent that as well as buying our own upgraded electrics, Jim also buy a fridge for Don and Yvonne. He didn't consider that this was Jim's investment money. I felt it was an unfair demand.

Right from the beginning of our marriage, I felt that Dick and Ella had not accepted me. Ella told me that she'd wanted to warn Jim not to marry me, and Dick could not handle that I'd been brought up to be responsible for my own decisions and the consequences of them. This had been a big part of my parents' training which was emphasised during my nursing career. When Dick made his demands about how Jim and I should use our own money, I insisted it was our business and we would do what we thought was right. This did not go well with Dick and he tried everything to make me do what he wanted. At one point he came around when Jim was not there, brought out his will, threw it on the table and said: "There's my will if you want to know what's in it."

I was horrified and threw it back to him. "I'm not the least interested in your will or what's in it. Jim and I will do what's right and work for what we get."

Poor Dick didn't know what to do with this daughter-in-law. Yvonne didn't have the same problem as me. I guess she was the first daughter-in-law and Ella and Dick cherished her. Yvonne had advised me the best way to handle them was to agree with everything they said and then do whatever you want. It worked well for her but I felt guilty, as it seemed I would be lying to them.

Eventually I couldn't take it anymore and decided to leave. Jim was beside himself and rang Mum who said, "let me talk to her." When I came to the phone she said, "Jen, don't be foolish, you can't leave Jim."

"I'm not leaving him Mum, he can come with me if he likes. I'm leaving his Father and Mother."

After some talk Mum promised to get an appointment with a minister they knew in Port Augusta. Jim and I went to talk with him about the problem. When we arrived at the manse, the first thing the minister said was he didn't want Jim to say anything. He wanted to hear what I had to say first and then he would listen to Jim. I told him what was troubling me, particularly the constant interference from Dick. He was out at our home before breakfast and stayed all day, expecting me to produce food for Jim, Don and him. He always walked into the house and even into my bedroom without asking. He would take anything that he wanted without asking. If I had things growing in the garden he would pick and take, not only what he wanted, but often extra to give to other people. He kept a tight hold on the money for the business and Jim had to account for every penny he was given for an allowance. Once I was milking my cow and found the bucket was falling to pieces, so I ask Jim if he could get another one. We usually used four-gallon honey tins bought from the local apiarist, and they only cost four shillings each, which was very cheap. When I told Jim we needed a new bucket, he went to his father and asked if it would be alright to get one. I couldn't believe that a married man of twenty-five would ask permission about four shillings for a milking bucket, but worse that his father should consider it and make the ultimate decision.

There were many other complaints. The Pastor could not believe I was being treated like this. Jim was sure his mother and father were always right. After hearing Jim's side of the story, the Pastor told him there are some things that, when a couple marry, a husband is responsible for, and that means it is not the place of his father to make the decisions and take control in this way.

I'm sure it must have been hard to hear this for the first

time, but Jim must have thought about the advice. Soon after, Dick and Ella came to the house. They immediately began to lay down the law about what could and couldn't be done. But this time Jim stood up to them.

"If you don't stop treating Jenny like this, we will leave," he said. "Even if we have to live in a tent, we will go."

It must have been a great shock to them. Only a couple of weeks later, Dick approached Jim to say he had decided to sell the property to him and to Don, and he was making arrangements straight away. The property would be mortgaged to Dick and Ella, and the sons would pay for it each year, giving them an income to live on. This was the best solution. Both Jim and Don now had to manage their own property and finances, and the arrangement worked well. The men continued to work together, helping each other all the time. Dick took on the role of a special hand to be there if they wanted extra help, or to just keep an eye on such things as weeds that needed spraying or any other little things that took his attention.

It was obvious that Jim still had a bit to learn before he would totally become master of his own home, but he was well on the way. Though, he did need to borrow my courage from time to time.

One dark night—as all nights tend to be, particularly on the farm—we'd just settled into bed. I was sitting up, putting rollers in my hair when something went bump in the night. Actually, to describe the sound more accurately, it sounded like the footsteps of somebody who was dragging something up the passage. My fertile imagination immediately concluded that something being dragged would have to be a dead body.

Both Jim and I froze, not quite willing to admit the fear that paralysed us, and hardly game to breathe either.

"What was that?" Jim tried to sound brave and nonchalant.

"I don't know," I answered, relieved that it wasn't just my imagination, and that my husband had heard it as well. "Go and have a look."

"What! Me?" He protested. "YOU GO!"

I was already aware of Jim's allergy to dark places. I'd chuckled on more than one occasion, having sent him out into the pitch-black night to get an orange, just because I felt like one. He'd always generously complied, after checking it was a desperate situation, and he would calmly disappear off the front veranda into the dark night. I could hear him bolt out to the tree and back again, until he'd hit the veranda. Then he'd walk in calmly with the orange in hand.

But facing an orange tree in the dark compared to a ruthless murderer, and a dead corpse—for the image continued to grow in our imagination—was a whole different ball game. Even with prompting and fluttering of the eyelids, I doubted I'd kid Jim into facing this unknown terror. Yet lying down to sleep knowing that someone was out there, lurking and dragging, was also out of the question. Facing the awful truth was better than not knowing at all.

"Oh, alright. I'll go!" I shrugged into my dressing gown and headed out of the bedroom. With torch in hand, I started down the long and very dark hallway in search of an explanation. Why didn't I just turn on the light, you may ask? Unfortunately, it was still in the days when the household electricity was run off a 32-volt generator and was therefore limited. The only light switch for that long, dark passage where all the monsters lurked, was at the kitchen end, away from the bedroom.

"Wait!" Jim called.

He's coming to take up his role, I thought. But, no.

"Wait," he repeated. "I don't want to stay here alone."

With Jim clinging to my dressing gown, we pursued the noise and found a large sheet of tar paper. The wind had blown it off the table on the back veranda and it was dragging along the ground as the wind rose and fell. To add to the noise, the back wire door was unlatched and the wind was blowing it open and closed, causing the butchers' hook hanging on the back to move back and forth. The banging on the door sounded like the phantom footsteps.

The homestead 1932

'Gumville' - our home from 1959 to 2023

14

THE PLAN

Like so many young people, we intended to have a family. We both wanted quite a few children. At first, we thought twelve would be good, but that number came down as we kept talking—from twelve to eight.

It wasn't long into our marriage when it seemed our plans were coming to life. Everyone was pleased to know a baby was on the way. One morning, about three or four months along, I had a terrible pain in my stomach. I knew something was wrong.

"I think I'm losing the baby," I said to Jim.

He thought for a while. "Could you milk the cows before you go back to bed?"

I was horrified. "Can't you understand?" I cried.

I got him to put the foot of the bed up on blocks so my legs would be elevated, and I rang the hospital. I was taken to the hospital and sure enough, our little baby was passed. We didn't know if it was a girl or a boy but we'd planned a boy's name—Craig.

We waited for some time before I was pregnant again,

and soon a baby girl came along. We welcomed our little Stephanie. She was delivered by Doctor Wheaton, who I'd worked with in my nursing days. I'd asked him if I could have a natural birth.

"Yes, if you'd like," he said. "You can scream and yell as much as you like, and I won't pay you any notice."

But I had no problems with the delivery. Jim wasn't with me for the birth—men were sent away from the birthing room in those days. Stephanie was already lying in my arms when he came in to see her. As soon as he entered the room, I wondered what was wrong with his face. It seemed to be swollen. I kept asking if he was all right. It took me a while to realise it was because he was smiling. I'd never seen such a big smile before.

Dick and Ella were delighted too, especially because Stephanie was such a plump and pretty baby.

"When Jim was born, he looked like a skun rabbit," Ella told me.

Dick, in particular, seemed to be gloating about Stephanie's size. Back when Jim was born, there was another woman from the next town over having a baby at the same time. Hers came out stocky and handsome, while Jim was two months premature.

Years later, there I was in hospital, and coincidentally, the stocky and handsome son of the woman from the next town over was there too, waiting for his child to be born.

The tables had turned—Jim had produced a plump baby, and it was the son's turn to have one that looked like a skun rabbit. Dick couldn't have been more pleased.

When number two baby arrived, Meredith was a smaller child with thick black hair just like her sister. The first thing I thought when she was born was, "Oh look at those eyes." Although she couldn't see properly, her eyes were as bright as a button and she seemed to be interested in everything. They brought her into me the first time and I looked at this little human who had this look of surprise, and I laughed. It wasn't long and the words came spilling out of the mouth as well.

Two little girls, and now another baby was on the way. Right from the start I was very unwell and had to have help in the house. I lost a lot of weight and things were not happy, but I made the distance. The time came for the child's birth, only she didn't want to come. It was almost two weeks after my due date, and we had been to church in the morning. I noticed the baby was very active. It must be happening soon. But the next day there was no movement at all. I rang Doctor Wheaton and he told me to come to the hospital. On examination he told me he feared the baby may be dead.

He delivered her that evening.

And he was right.

The beautiful little girl, so like her sisters, lay there with no life in her.

Carolyn.

My heart was broken.

I spent the mandatory time in hospital with people telling me I needed to put it out of my mind.

"There will be other children," they tried to comfort me.

The Wilmington CWA filled my room with flowers and were so kind, but I felt as if I'd been punched in the face.

I came home after a week. Mum came to stay with me, and I went back to life as if it was normal, but nothing felt normal. Then, on one particular day, it seemed like every little thing would become an argument. It came to a head when Jim and I disagreed on something ridiculous—an argument about which direction the creek ran. It was such a silly thing, but it was what I needed, because Jim was being stubborn about it and eventually I burst into tears, and didn't stop. It caused me to let go of all the sadness and sorrow in my heart and I was able to cry, and cry, and cry for my dear little baby, Carolyn Jennette.

It wasn't long and the next one was on the way. I was only three months and once again I was on the way to the hospital to try to save my baby, and once again I failed. I was in theatre in no time, but it was not quick enough. This time the doctor was a locum, a very nice man. After it was over he explained all about it, sitting beside the bed and holding my hand. But my attention was fixed on a figure that was standing just behind and a little to the side of him. This man was dressed in white, had long hair and a beard, and when he came into the room an aura of peace followed and filled the room. He didn't speak, but he didn't need too. I was devastated at the loss of another child, but I somehow felt the presence of Jesus, and I felt His comfort.

It began to seem as if we would only have our two little girls, and we found delight in them as they grew. Something that brought us a lot of pleasure during this time was a little horse called Tumbleweed. Tumbleweed was a Shetland pony we bought for Stephanie as she was getting on very well with her riding. Little did we know these Shetlands were the trickiest things you could wish for. We still had Laddie who was an exceptionally quiet horse, and the girls learnt to ride on him. But Tumbleweed had the bad habit of giving little sudden bucks. He really had the knack of throwing his rider off. The day we brought him home, my dad—who was enjoying his role as Grandpa—was there. Being an excellent horseman, he was delighted to be involved in Stephanie's first ride. He lined Tumbleweed up and began to show Stephanie how to vault onto a horse bareback. Everyone stood back while Grandpa launched himself up and straight over the top of Tumbleweed. He landed with a thump on the ground on the other side.

"He's a bit smaller than I thought," Dad said.

Though I had almost given up hope, as time passed, I found I was pregnant again. This time everything seemed to go well. Doctor Wheaton was very watchful, and checked the baby all the time. I was at the point the doctor thought the baby should arrive, but he wouldn't let it go overtime again, so I went to hospital to have an induction. Then we waited a few days, and nothing. I had a second induction, and again we waited, and nothing. Then the nurse came in to see me and said, "Doctor wants to know if you would mind having another induction on April Fool's Day?"

"Oh, let's get on with it," I said. That's how Tim came to be born on April 1st. Knowing his quick wit and sense of humour, it seems to me it was the right thing to do.

But sadness knocked at our door.

After waiting all these years for a grandson, just twenty-five days later, my dad, Arthur Hamlyn, died.

It happened suddenly. Dad had only just retired and they'd bought their first home in Wilmington. It seemed as if he was finally ready to settle, after years of moving from place to place in his attempts to forget what he'd seen in war. But it was not to be. He had a heart attack on the 8th of April. They thought he would recover, and he was due to be sent home—but on the day he was to be released, he passed away, right at dawn. It was the 25th April, 1966. ANZAC Day.

Before my dad left us, he had the opportunity of nursing his grandson—only once—but it was the thing he'd wanted more than anything in the world.

Two years later, the next little lady came along but the delivery was quite different to the others. She was a darling little baby who grew into a beautiful lady, but we had trouble in the beginning. Jim had made up his mind this baby was a boy. I made many suggestions of girl's names but he was determined and refused to consider a girl's name. I wanted especially to have Ann in her name if it was a girl, as I knew my name would not be carried on and Ann was my second name, so I selected Rose-Ann. Jim would not consider it at all. Then came the great day when I was off to hospital. With so much trouble previously, it was always a bit daunting, but everything seemed to be going well this time. Until right at the time of delivery, when I began to haemorrhage. That sent everyone into a spin, and as I lost a lot of blood, I began to lose consciousness. After it was all over, they got me cleaned up and into a nice warm bed where I lay quietly, feeling so weak and awful, but happy that my baby was alright. At last, they let Jim come in to sit with me and as I floated in and out of consciousness, I managed to make little statements. "Well, it's a girl, what are you going to do now? She has to have a name."

"All right," he answered. "It can be Lee-Ann."

And with that I lost consciousness again. By the time I was awake and with it, Lee-Ann had been named. Our neighbours, the Dicksons, were delighted; Leanne Dickson was sure the baby had been named especially for her, never mind the difference in spelling. So everyone was happy.

We'd had seven pregnancies and had four children, and I was beginning to think that was enough. But there was a little niggle that said, keep going, and when I found I was pregnant again I was sure it was God's will.

This time I found I was very tired and uncomfortable. My baby often seemed to be laying in an awkward position for me and I couldn't do anything about it until it decided to move. On one occasion there was a knock at the door and in came two or three boys from the church youth group. They were horrified to find me leaning over between the table and a traymobile beside it. I was totally unable to move or stand up. The baby was moving around though, and eventually I could stand up again. When the time came for the baby to be delivered, the baby decided that it would just lay there and rest a while on an angle that couldn't be moved, so I just had to lay there too, trying to push him along. Finally, our baby boy, Andrew, made his appearance, a fine strapping young man. I had this very definite feeling that this was the last one to make up the family. Phew!

And even though none of it had gone according to the plan Jim and I made when we were newlyweds, I can't help but feel it went the right way, after all.

The family complete 1970

15

HOSPITAL HANGOVER

As previously mentioned, in those days, once a woman was married, she was no longer able to be employed as a nurse. But that didn't mean what I'd learned had been wasted. In these small country towns everyone knows everyone, and if you need help, everyone is there to help you. Because I'd recently been nursing, if there was any need for a helping hand in the health arena, I'd be called on. Unfortunately for me, what was needed was an undertaker. We had an undertaker who worked in the area, but he refused to deal with anyone who'd died at home. He didn't have to deal with anyone who died in hospital either, as that was part of the nurses' job. I wondered what circumstances were required for him to actually do his job. But because of his rules, when there was a death in the Melrose area, Dr Wheaton would ring me. I would go to the home of the person who'd died, Dr Wheaton would give me instructions, and then leave me to deal with the grieving family, as well as lay out the body of the deceased ready for burial. I couldn't do this on my own of course, but fortunately, my neighbour Janice Moulton was also an ex-nurse, so I used to call on her to help me.

Normally we'd start with the grieving family. We'd ask them for everything we'd need—things to wash the body and the clothes the family wanted them dressed in. Then we'd ask if they'd make a pot of tea, and put plenty of sugar in it. We found that if they had to bustle about making tea, it helped them to cope. Then we'd get them to drink the tea, which would also give them a boost. Several people told me afterwards it was the best thing we could have done for them. After that, Jan and I would go to work and get everything ready for the body to be collected.

I know I was helping, and I know I did a good job, but I hated having to do it. It got that way that I would dread hearing the phone ring any time after 10 o'clock at night, as it was sure to be Dr Wheaton.

This went on for a number of years until I was pregnant with Carolyn. On one occasion I was called into an accident in the town to a family who lived on the edge of town. One day, the father had come out of their home and crossed the road to walk into town. His little daughter came running after, wanting to go with him. Just at that moment, one of the older ladies was driving, very slowly, along the road. She always drove slowly. But this meant the little girl wasn't worrying about the car, and she ran straight out in front and was knocked down. Everyone rushed up and soon had her laying on the bed in Mrs Slee's house, two houses from where the accident happened. They rang the Doctor immediately, but it was to no avail. The child had died. I was called in to see if I could attend to the body, but I was pregnant with a child of my own, and I couldn't bear it. I asked them to get someone else, which they did.

I only attended one other death that happened at home,

after that. That was our neighbour Mr Clarke. I was very pregnant, and so I had to arrange for a couple of other people to do the physical part of the job while I told them what to do. After this incident, it was organised to get the bodies over to the hospital so the nurses could deal with them. Now all Jan and I had to do was pick up any people who had been in an accident. I remember Jan ringing me to say another neighbour had come too fast around the corner and had come off his motorbike right in front of their house, and so I raced up there to help. Thankfully it wasn't too bad an injury, and he got through just fine. It wasn't the first time this neighbour and his motorbike had been parted—and it wasn't the last. We were on call like this though, and had to attend some serious incidents until the St Johns Ambulance was started and we didn't have to be involved any more.

During this time of my life, it sometimes seemed I was surrounded by death. I lost my dear baby Carolyn, my father and had two other miscarriages, and every time the phone rang at that dreadful hour, I knew there had been more grief.

But there is always a silver lining if you can find it. Even though it turned out to be a miserable time, I managed to purchase the cutest little bulldog as a pet for myself. Everyone who came to visit was frightened when they saw him because of his breed, but he had a lovely nature. As usual he took a liking to Jim and followed him everywhere. I always found it amusing when Jim was working a paddock going round and round on the tractor, the little dog following. He wasn't able to keep up with the tractor because of his short legs, but he would keep level with Jim, turning small circles in the middle of the paddock.

Thankfully, the duties of the doctor were not always about tragedy and loss. We were lucky in those days that Doctor Wheaton would make house calls to some of his more needy patients, and he would hold clinic in each town. Our turn in Melrose was Tuesdays and Fridays. On Tuesday he had morning clinic at Melrose, then went on to Wilmington for the afternoon, and on Friday he held clinic at Wilmington in the morning and Melrose in the afternoon. But 'clinic' did not mean a fancy medical building to hold appointments. When we were first married, Doctor Wheaton held the clinic in the Mount Remarkable Hotel. These days, there is a doorway from the bar to the Nook, but it didn't exist when Doctor Wheaton held clinic there. There was an outside entrance to that end of the building, so you didn't have to go through the bar. The door came into a wide passage with seats for you to sit and wait your turn to see the doctor. On one end of the passage was a door to the doctor's consultation room, and on the other, a door straight into the hotel. It wasn't very private, but good enough. The only problem—as with all country towns—everyone knew everyone else's business. For example, a visit of a newlywed to the doctor's clinic could only mean one thing. In the early days, I had to see Doctor Wheaton as I had a moth in my ear. He was delighted to realise that, despite the keen attention of the people in the waiting passage, my issue was not pregnancy-related. "This will make the locals talk," he chuckled. "They'll be counting the months now."

After a while, the clinic moved to the RSL room with Doctor Wheaton consulting in the kitchen. Everyone who went to see him in the clinic would arrive at the same time he was due to arrive, though he was always late, so you just sat and waited. Patients noted which order they'd come into the waiting room and had their visits in turn. If they were down the list a bit, they would arrange with the patient next to them to save their spot so they could go over to Prests to do their shopping.

If something happened and it wasn't a Tuesday or Friday, we could only access a consult by travelling to Booleroo Centre. We'd usually make the most of this trip, and get something from the shop. But other times the long drive to see the doctor was done with urgency. I recall one occasion when my daughter, Meredith, was about sixteen. We were in the ute driving a herd of cattle along Three Chain Road coming from Willowmear, moving slowly to let the cows graze on the side of the road as we went along. Meredith had been walking beside the ute to push some of the stragglers along, and as she hopped back in, she pulled the door shut; only her hand was still on the top of the door. It shut firmly, leaving her fingers sticking out one side. I tried desperately to open the door but it was jammed over the fingers. I drove at top speed to Melrose, and stopped at the garage to see if they could help me prise the door open, and praise the Lord, a few of the men got some tyre leavers and between them they were able to spring it open enough for her to pull her hand out. Poor hand. It was as squashed as it could be, right across the knuckles of her right hand. I was mortified. I thought she would never be able to play the piano again. We finally made it to the doctor, who took her hand in his, and carefully moved each joint. When he had finished, he said, "I don't think there is even anything broken." And there wasn't. I couldn't believe it. Why did it have no injury at all? I can only put it down to the fact that we both prayed hard all the way to Booleroo.

Then there was the other real disaster. Tim was about three years old, and I'd left him with Yvonne for the morning while I took the older two for an appointment. It was a nice day, so Yvonne set Tim up on the veranda with some toys to play with while she was working in the garden. All was quiet and pleasant until Yvonne's big red kelpie dog suddenly flew up the veranda and attacked Tim. He bit him viciously about the head and face, tearing his left ear from his head and slashing his throat from the ear almost to his chin, leaving a bite right in the middle of his cheek. Yvonne contacted me and I came quickly to the scene. He was wrapped in a blanket and I put him in the car and said, "Call the doctor and let him know I'm coming!"

I left at top speed.

Unbeknownst to me, this particular Saturday, Doctor Wheaton had calculated the risk of having anyone need treatment and had decided it was unlikely. He'd arranged for another young man to look after the practise for a few hours so he could have some time off. This young man was a relative of one of the local farmers and had only just finished his training and was not expecting to have to deal with an emergency. When I got to the doctor's surgery, I was the only patient there, and I was shown straight in. The new doctor came in and I told him what had happened as he looked at Tim's injuries. He stood and looked around a bit, then he went to one cupboard, then another. It was quite obvious he didn't know where anything was or what he could use. After a few minutes of this I decided to take a hand.

"I think in a case like this Doctor Wheaton would go to hospital to do the job," I said.

The relief on his face was obvious. "Oh yes," he said. So I wrapped Tim up and put him back in the car, while the poor doctor called ahead. When I arrived at the hospital they had everything out and ready to deal with the problem. That young doctor rose to the occasion then and did a wonderful job on Tim's face. It was as good as a plastic surgeon. But it took Tim a long time to be able to trust dogs after that.

It was always good to know we had such a good doctor in Doctor Wheaton who we could call on day or night. I remember my youngest, Andrew, only about four months old at the time, was obviously sick. I had him in the crib beside our bed, but I couldn't stop him crying, so I rang Doctor Wheaton. I soon had him over at the hospital where they found the baby had meningitis. This was a worrying few weeks and for some time I had to go over to the hospital to feed him. Poor little fellow couldn't bear me holding him in my arms so I had to let him lie so there was no pressure on his head. I'd always had a rule with the children that we did not have dummies, but the staff soon had a dummy for Andrew, which he loved. When he came home, I found he would not settle without it, and worse, he insisted on having honey on it as well. It took me some time to break him of the habit.

During this time locals were making moves to get a branch of the St. John's Ambulance Service started at Booleroo. I thought it worthwhile to be part of the ambulance service, so I signed up. We had regular nights for training and I would often visit organisations as a speaker. We serviced all the local events including all the shows in the area.

One we regularly attended was the Carrieton Rodeo. I always enjoyed attending this event. In contrast to other events, where there was very little to do, the rodeo provided constant activity.

We set ourselves up in the shed provided for us, then a couple of the men would go out into the ring, ready to help any rider who might be injured. The men often came back to say they couldn't convince the cowboys to come in to be checked over, but in time some would be knocked out and have no choice but to be brought in on the stretcher. The cowboys were always grateful for the help, but they'd be up and back out there as soon as they could.

On one occasion, a call was put out over the speaker for us to attend to a case. The men asked me to go and move a car that had parked across the track, blocking access for our ambulance. I drove down to the car, found the owner and asked if he would move his vehicle. He flicked his hand at me and said, "The keys are in it. You can do it." Then he and some of his friends gathered around to watch.

Do they think I can't drive their car? I got into the big Chevvy and reached over to the keys. Only then did I see a huge brown snake, curled up on the floor next to me and staring right at me. My blood ran cold and I froze until I realised it was dead. So, this was what they were all interested in. My reaction could not have been more disappointing for them as I expertly threw the car into gear and drove it forward. Leaving the car in a hurry, I went to the ambulance and went on my merry way. Ha!

Another time, while working in the shed, the speaker sounded: "It looks like a car has turned over at the top of the hill. Someone get help." The crew jumped into action to get the ambulance up to the top of the hill while the local doctor, who was at the rodeo on his day off, called me to drive with him to the scene. The ute had turned over while the driver had been on his way to the rodeo. He'd been steering with one hand, leaning the other arm through the open window while he smoked his cigarette. A truck had passed him so close that it shaved the side of his ute and knocked it, causing it to turn over—taking the driver's elbow that had been sticking out the window, stripping it of all flesh as it dragged along the ground. When we got there the doctor immediately went to work, doing the usual things to stop the loss of blood. I was surprised as I'd thought there would be blood pouring everywhere, but there wasn't.

"We have to work quickly," the doctor explained to me.

"The body is in shock and has shut down, so the blood's not flowing, but it will start very soon."

And it did. It was a bloody mess, but we got the job done.

In the end, just because I got married, my interest and participation in all-things-hospital never went away. And it was wonderful to have Doctor Wheaton to work with, whether I was a nurse, a stand-in undertaker, an ambo volunteer, or a mother who had to help a new doctor work out what to do.

Doctor Wheaton went on consulting at the RSL rooms for many years until he retired and the practise was taken over. The consulting rooms moved to various places after that. At one time they were in the post office. Sadly the various new doctors objected to having to consult at Melrose, and so eventually the mobile clinics were shut down. From then on, all patients had to go to the medical clinic at Booleroo Centre. At time of writing, that's still the case.

It has been hard, over the years, to see our rural towns change from thriving communities, to ones where the services are barely hanging on. I would love services to come back to all the country towns with the support they once had, but as I'm writing this, all I can hope for is that the clinic and hospital at Booleroo Centre, at least, stay protected.

16

MELROSE COMMUNITY LIFE

After Dad died, Mum found it very hard to settle. She would visit me on the farm, and when it came time to go home, she would say how she hated putting the key in the door at the Wilmington house. They'd only been there a short time before Dad died, and she had no memories there. Marg was working at the Wilmington Hotel at the time and would often be home late. Mum seemed to be getting more and more uptight. Eventually her blood pressure had risen so high that her nose was constantly bleeding, and several times Doctor had to cauterize it to stop the flow of blood. She was very unhappy, and Marg and I didn't know what to do about it. Then we came up with the idea of a Granny Flat beside our house. Jim was in agreement, so the plan was put into action.

Mum and Marg came with me to select a transportable house. We sat in the office with the assistant, selected the floor plan, then went through it carefully, asking if some of the features could be changed. They accepted our alterations, and later told us they were going to make our updated version their new official plan, as it was so much better than the original one.

So, the cottage was bought and transported to the site we selected, right next door to our farm house. There was a row of bushes and trees between our houses to make it private. Mum and Marg were very happy to move into the cottage which I named Shalom Cottage. Being so close, Mum was on hand to help me with the house and children while still having a private life of her own. The children loved running over there after school to get their biscuit and play games with her. Andrew, especially, considered it a holiday to stay at Grandma's. He used to pack a bag with his clothes and walk across the garden to Grandma's for the night. They would have tea, play a game of canasta, then to bed. The next morning, Andrew would get up early, pack his case, and be home by breakfast time.

With Mum joining us in Melrose, we were well and truly settled in the community and fully involved in the town's activities.

Of course, my father-in-law Dick had instructions on how we were to do this.

"You will shop at *both* the grocery shops in town," he'd informed me as soon as I was married. "One month at Prests', the next month at Christensons'."

I did this religiously, every month. The other place I was to support was Young's Corner, where we could buy our vegetables, café goods, and fresh bread.

Mr Young baked his bread every Tuesday and Friday, and most town activities were scheduled to synchronize with bread day. Why go into town for one task when you could attend to everything on your list at once?

On Fridays there was a town-wide afternoon tea. There was a roster, and each organisation would take turns running it—the Methodist Church, the Hospital Auxiliary, the Country Women's Association, the Anglican Ladies and the Mothers' and Babies Health Association. Each group, when rostered, was responsible for providing the food, setup and cleanup, and proceeds raised went to that organisation for their use.

The afternoon teas were held at the back of our lovely big town hall, known as the Institute. The townsfolk wouldn't come in the front—they'd wait until someone rang the big bell at the top of the path, and then the whole town it seemed, would make their way to the kitchen door and set themselves up in the dining area. The cost was minimal, and you'd get a cup of tea with hot water from the copper, and as much food as you'd like. When it was my turn to work with whichever organisation I was supporting, I would cook all morning and take a big container full of cakes, slices and sandwich fillings. Avis Clarke always arrived with a suitcase full of food, and most of the other members did the same. But there were some who found an easy way out. A few ladies brought a cooked chicken which they claimed was for sandwich fillings, but at the end of the day they always took leftovers from everyone else's cooking, free of charge. Then there was one contributor who brought a pound of butter which had been softened so that it could be spread on the sandwiches, and that was all. But thankfully there were many contributors, so no one ever left hungry.

There was one older couple who always came for the afternoon tea, and every time they would survey the table and pick the area that had the most goodies on it, then sit down and eat as if it was their evening meal. They never donated anything, though they could well afford it. My Mum used to get so cross about it that she'd wait until they were seated, and then she would put her food right up the other end of the table, out of their reach, taking care to move some of the nicer goodies like the cream puffs, while she was doing it.

Market day was held on Fridays as well, so it was good to get all the people from the market to come to the afternoon tea. My daughter Meredith recalled visiting the stock markets as a young child:

"There were the times when I was allowed the privilege of going to the stock sales. This was fun for a while, but tagging along for hour upon endless hour, chewing dust kicked up by the farmers' boots, swatting at annoying flies, wondering what on earth these men were mumbling about as they looked at pens of sheep and cattle, eventually became a chore. I soon learned to sympathise with the sheep dogs who sat listlessly in the tray of the ute, waiting to go home."

Luckily, our afternoon teas could provide some respite from the boredom.

The Institute was the site for a lot of town events in those days. Concerts were quite popular, and travelling shows would perform and bring big crowds. One of the town favourites was Harold Raymond. Harold Raymond was a violinist who was totally blind, yet he made the instrument talk. Every time he came to Melrose, the entire town came out to see him. There were always several other artists who came as supporting acts, and it was an excellent variety concert.

Another group that toured occasionally was the Metropolitan Male Voice Choir. These gentlemen were top singers and their productions were very professional. Once, their piano accompanist was a girl who was totally blind, and her playing was beautiful. These events always inspired me, seeing people excel despite living with disabilities.

Besides these travelling entertainments, the local

community held a strawberry fete each year in November. Everyone worked hard in the months leading up to the fete, producing all kinds of things for the stalls. The craft stall featured handiwork the ladies had made. I always bought my aprons at that stall. There was a lolly stall ladened with all kinds of homemade sweets—fudge, honeycomb, sugared almonds, toffees, and coconut ice. The lucky dip stall had two boxes prepared with toys and gifts—one box for boys and one for girls. And of course at the strawberry stall you could buy a plate of cut-up strawberries with ice-cream and cream, sprinkled with icing sugar. People arrived early so they could make their purchases, often things they could use for Christmas gifts. After a given time, all selling would stop and the concert of local artists presented. Unfortunately, as years went by, it became difficult to get local artists, so the primary school was asked to produce the concert. It was not quite the same standard of entertainment listening to an evening of little tackers singing their nursery rhymes or playing the one-page songs they'd learned from the town's piano teacher, Vera Fuller. But it was an experience for them.

The Melrose Show remained the height of our calendar year. My mother-in-law, Ella, seemed to be preparing for the show all year round. Although we'd had a bad start, eventually she learned that we could get on well together. In fact, as Ella got older, she often rang me to get advice on her health, or other things she needed help with. But she remained the master at gardening. Ella was known for the flowers she entered into the various competitions, and I learned from her that I must get the roses pruned in July and no later, as that would bring the best blooms for the show. It is a practice I kept throughout my life. I was also shown how to select the fruit for preserving so that it sat correctly in the jar, ready for judging, and to be careful when making jam and chutney, to make sure the outside of the jar was washed clean and not sticky. As show day drew nearer, the best eggs were collected and put aside. Ella was a proactive grandmother. As the children got older, she would set aside some of her own goods for the children to enter into the competitions. She had a large biscuit tin of unshelled almonds which turned up in the appropriate competition every year, but with a different Bishop child's name on it.

In the early days we always had our Hereford stud cattle to show, but after we sold the stud, we only had a couple of house milking cows, including our little Jersey, Mrs Moo. There was no question: we had to enter her as we couldn't let a Melrose show go by without an entry in the cattle section. There we were with our one little cow while all the big breeders had their very best stock on show. What a surprise when the judges selected Mrs Moo as the grand champion. There she was leading the grand parade while all the others had to follow. There were a lot of grumpy faces that year. It was a good year all round for us. Stephanie won the miss show girl competition, and in the same year Lee-Ann won the junior miss show girl.

Eventually, I became as involved in the shows as Ella and Dick. At first I was mostly with the horses, but as time went on I took on the role of co-convenor of the dog section with one of the old farmers. Some other men made fun of him because he had some strange ways as a result of his service in World War One, but I got on well with him. I learned so much about the dogs—the different breeds, what they liked, but most of all, how the owners handled their dogs. In time, the old farmer left and I ran the dog section alone. I did this for several years, until the decision was made to discontinue the dog section and have sheep dog trials instead.

But my participation wasn't over yet. Jim was elected

president of the Mount Remarkable Agricultural Show Society in 1988 and I discovered that there was a special role for the president's wife as well. Apparently it was the duty of the president's wife to clean all the toilets.

"WHAT!" I exclaimed when Jim announced this to me.

I've never believed that one's spouse should be expected to take part in club activities just because their spouse did, and I was certainly not going to clean the toilets, and I told them in no uncertain manner. As a result, the show society decided to hire someone to be the cleaner. That position has now grown into a full-time caretaker of the show grounds. Spouses of future presidents—you're welcome.

OVER THE YEARS, Jim was not only known for being the President of the Melrose Show. Occasionally he managed to develop a few other reputations as well.

Jim and I continued the farming work as we'd always done for years, but as with everything, the government always has to have a say.

In this case, the government brought in a law that if you had cattle of six months or over, you had to have an identifying tail tag when it came time to sell at the stock markets. This was to help identify any animal that was found to have a disease. The tag could then be traced back to the original owner.

When we had the 1982 drought, things became so bad we had to get rid of our stock. Bit by bit, the commercial herd we'd built up had to go. Jim put the appropriate tail tags on the cattle but found he was about half a dozen tags short. To buy the tags you had to get them in lots of 100, so as we were quitting the last of our cattle at this sale, he went and asked our neighbour if he could use a few of his—just to finish off the last few calves. That was okay, and Jim soon had the animals tagged and ready for sale.

Unbeknownst to Jim, the rules had been changed *again*, and now you had to have tags on animals from three months old. When the inspector came along and saw there were young stock with no tags, he went to the adult cows to find out who the cattle belonged to. In doing that, he discovered that some of our stock had one tag, and some had a different tag. He immediately wrote out a fine for the owner—Jim Bishop. He'd just finished writing it up when Jim came along and explained the situation. The inspector said, "Oh I wish I'd known, but I can't do anything about it now. I've already written out the fine." As a result, Jim had to go to court in Port Pirie.

There he was, lined up with all those who had committed a crime of some kind.

"Do you have a lawyer?" the judged asked, when his name was called.

"No," Jim replied.

"What do you want to do about legal counsel?"

"I'll defend myself."

"Do you realise the seriousness of this crime?" The stern-faced judge asked.

"No," Jim replied.

As the judge turned to ask the clerk of the court what the charge meant, it appeared he probably didn't know the seriousness of the charge either.

Jim was allowed to tell the story of having to quit his animals due to the drought, and by the time he had finished the judge was nearly crying. He fined Jim thirty dollars and that was it.

Until the family decided to have fun at his expense.

Whenever anyone wanted to stir him up, all they had to do was say "Jim the crim."

Apparently, this wasn't our family's only brush with the law. Years later I was talking to Liz Bishop, who was laid up with an injured back. She'd been looking through some old Register Papers, and found an announcement of someone named George Bishop, sentenced to prison for cattle rustling. I couldn't believe it. I did some further research to see if it was *our* George Bishop. I was aware there'd been another one who arrived in Australia at exactly the same time as ours. After further investigation it was Jim's great-uncle. Apparently, George Bishop was in the employ of a farmer from Wilmington, who had a lucrative business rustling cattle. However, his unfortunate workmen were the ones who got caught, and they were jailed for two years in Port Augusta. Meanwhile, the farmer went on to Melrose and become a pillar of the church.

It had always been a mystery to me when I was writing the Bishop History—there was nothing recorded about George for two years of his life. His family told me he'd gone to Western Australia and they had not kept in contact until he returned to South Australia. The only question I have is where do you think the Western Australia border is? I fancy it might be just south of Port Augusta at the Port August jail.

So it turned out Jim was not the only Bishop who had to front up to court!

EVEN THOUGH JIM is not particularly sporty, he was community minded and a ready volunteer. If any of the sporting clubs were looking for members he usually put up his hand to play. That's how he played for the Murray Town tennis team. During that time he used to wear a pair of grey shorts, but he was always having trouble with them coming loose and starting to fall down during a match. He told people that when his opponents saw it, they missed the ball.

Jim also took his turn at football. Lined up with the other players, Jim always seemed as if his legs were too short. He used to tell our daughter Lee-Ann that it was good to have short legs as you could run faster. He played for Melrose, in the B grade.

Finally, he found the game that suited his special talent—table tennis. He was always very good at it, and wanted a table at home to practise on. One year, I saw a painting I liked, so I said that I'd give it to him for his Christmas.

"If you do, I'll give you a table tennis table," he replied.

I didn't follow through, but he did, so I got the table tennis table. I never played on it, but all the children and grandchildren learned to play. Jim was really very good. Every time we had a visitor, he'd get them to play and try to beat him. But he was rarely beaten.

Luckily this was a much nicer thing to be known for, as opposed to 'Jim the Crim'.

Mum's transportable granny flat - 1970

17

THE HOLIDAY TRADITION

Right from the beginning, Jim and I made it a habit to have annual holidays. I guess I felt it was necessary. I'd been taught at the Adelaide Hospital that everyone *had* to have two weeks holiday a year, and I knew the RAH never gave their workers anything they didn't have to. So, even though we were farmers and set our own hours, we organised to have our two weeks after harvest each year.

One little break, we went to Adelaide to farewell Margaret before she left to go to England for a time. She was going to see a specialist to try to get help after the results of the tumour removal operation that both saved and damaged her, all those years ago. While we were down in city, I decided to get some new clothes as mine were getting shabby. I went shopping with my old nursing friend, Janet, and I bought a nice light-green chiffon dress designed with a Roman look. Just to add something special I bought a lovely evening fox-fur. We were staying at Jan's place, and when we came home, her husband, Ron, was discussing the evening meal with us. We hadn't planned anything special, so Ron asked Jim if he liked Chinese food. We'd never tried anything like that, so they suggested we go out to a Chinese restaurant for a meal and then to a night-club, something else we'd never done before. We agreed. Didn't I feel flash that night, eating new and exotic food and dancing on a small dance floor in the club. That was a once off.

When Stephanie was about two, we stayed with Jan and Ron for some of the holiday. While there we did our best to let Stephanie experience new things. Just being at the beach was exciting for her, as she'd never seen the sea before and had never had the chance to go in for a swim. We also went to the West Beach Airport to show Stephanie the planes coming in. But her real delight was when we went to the zoo, seeing animals she'd only experienced in pictures. The shine was taken off that visit for me when I considered the way the animals were kept, shut away from their natural habitat in the wild. The other thing we did was to take her to see the neon lights in the city, and then to Semaphore to enjoy the fairground there. There were a lot of sideshows and she had a ride on the beautiful merry-go-round, a toy train and a spaceship. We all enjoyed our outing to the fair.

It was the first of many annual holidays. Mostly, our holidays ended without a hitch, though once, we came home from our time away to find there had been terrible dust storms. The place was filthy. Dust storms were not unusual in our area during the summer. Having a very old house, the dust gets in at every nook and cranny. We were quite used to it—we just weren't expecting it on this occasion.

The threat of dust storm wasn't going to stop us from going away. In early years it was only visits to friends and relatives, such as Jim's Auntie Elsie and Uncle Warren, who lived along the River Murray. Eventually we were able to borrow my second-cousin's holiday shack at Sellicks Beach.

He was happy for us to have the shack for two weeks and four days each year, and as it was near the beach, it was just right for us. There was plenty of room for the kids to play, with a pristine beach that wasn't too deep. The interesting thing about these holidays was that every year, without fail, as soon as we arrived at the shack it would start to rain. We'd always ring my cousins Rod and Joy and ask them to bring their kids down and have lunch with us. They always brought cooked chicken with them, and we enjoyed it a lot – Melrose didn't have any places to buy chicken as a take-away, so this was a treat. When they arrived, Rod would always greet us with, "I told Joy you lot were down, it's started raining."

The other place we went to for several years was Rapid Bay. Pat and Snow Anderson, old friends of Mum and Dad's, had a Granny flat next to their house. It was quite small—two rooms with beds that came out of the cupboards to be set up at night. But we bought a big two-roomed tent and used that as our bedroom and holidayed in the cottage. The cottage was right on the beach front, and it was just lovely for our kids. Snow very kindly supplied us with fishing lines and the know-how about fishing. We spent a lot of time on the jetty fishing for Tommy Ruffs and with quite a lot of success, we had fish for tea just about every night. Snow and Pat's son had a catamaran. We occasionally had a chance to sail with him. It was also nice for me to go for drives around the district and see the area that had been my childhood home when we lived at Delamere.

One year we hired a flat in Barmera. Tim was just a small baby and could only just sit up, so we always had to have someone with him. Just in front of our flat was an area closed off from the river, so the children were safe. This was where they had their learn-to-swim lessons. It was quite a pleasant place to stay, but we only went there once.

On one rare occasion, Jim and I went on a holiday on our own. Margaret had just been away on a tour and recommended it to me. It was a Christian bus trip put on by one of the church organisations—three weeks travelling around New Zealand. The couple who ran it were a Baptist couple and had been doing it for some years. Margaret made arrangements for us to take the trip, and we arranged for the younger children to stay with Jan and Ron, while Stephanie and Meredith stayed at home with Mum keeping an eye on them from her cottage.

We first met our hosts when we landed in New Zealand, having flown from Sydney. He was a retired Baptist Minister, and he introduced us to the other members of the party, two coaches full plus our drivers. Then we were taken to our rooms in Wellington where the trip was to start.

The next morning, we set off to go to the top of the island, Auckland. All the way along the Māori bus driver kept apologising for the lack of green grass as they'd been in drought. It was quickly apparent that drought in New Zealand was different to drought in Australia. We were amazed at the beautiful fields of green feed!

In Auckland we visited an extinct volcano, and then a beautiful park at night, all lit with coloured lights, water features and a stage where performances were held. We were also introduced to the biggest ice-creams you ever saw—a double cone which had enough ice-cream to fill it and then another two scoops on top. It was huge, but we soon learned that on this tour, everything had lots of cream and ice-cream on it.

We left Auckland and as we travelled down the East side of the island, our host explained the story of three volcanoes further down the coast. One of them was Mt Egmont. She described it as a beautiful volcano, but it always had a cap of snow and its head was always in the clouds. It was rare that you could see the whole mountain. I'd shared with her that I believed we'd been blessed enough for God to give us this holiday, so I was determined to see the best of everything.

"It will be beautiful anyway, even though you won't see the top of it," she said.

Everyone was watching carefully and then suddenly there it was, as clear and as beautiful as she had said, except there was no cloud on it. We could see right from the top with smoke curling up from it. The host watched me carefully after that.

We went down to Rotarua where the ground was actually shaking, it's so unstable, and we walked along a boardwalk which went over the boiling mud. We were instructed to make sure we all stayed together as we walked across to the bus that would be waiting on the other side. When we got to the bus and got on we found that two ladies (in their eighties) were missing. That put everyone in a tizz, and so a couple were sent back over the boardwalk while the bus went back to the other side to try to find them. They found them where the bus had first dropped us. They said they didn't feel like walking across the mud and so didn't go with the rest of us.

Another place we visited was Coronet Peak. There was a small hut which housed the workings of a chair lift which folk could get on, two by two, and be taken to the top of the mountain. This seemed about twice as far as we had already gone in the car. With the help of the attendants, each couple got onto the slowly moving chairlift and closed a bar across the front of them, then were slowly lifted to the top. As we were ascending it felt quite eerie, just us and masses of space with total silence. Jim began inspecting the chairlift, looking up to the runners and commenting on them.

"I wonder what kind of job they did on the welding?" he muttered to me.

I didn't want to know.

Unbeknownst to us, our two little ladies were in the chairlift behind us. When it was their turn to get on, they were very slow and didn't get the bar across the front of them closed properly. They were quite unaware that they were not safely hooked in, until they made it to the other side.

We were booked to take a small plane up onto the Fox Glacier but this was delayed when the plane had trouble with the group before us. It had gotten them up to the ice, but it couldn't bring them back. Apparently, they'd landed and got out to experience the snow. When they reboarded, one of the men took his soaked shoes and socks off. Then the pilot began the take-off but the plane would not lift off the ground. At the last moment, they had to open the door and jump out, leaving the plane to go over the cliff. We didn't hear how the man with no shoes or socks got on, but it was some time before they could get another plane up to them. That night we were sitting looking out our window and saw an aircraft coming in carrying the crashed plane beneath. We were booked to go up the next morning. We did go up and it was quite an experience, but one I could have done without.

That wasn't our last adventure. We were near the end of our wonderful holiday and the last big thing we were to do was a trip into Milford Sound—a large lake in between the mountains with waterfalls all around the outside. We went down to the boats and everyone selected which boat they would go on. The tour took us for a good look at the walls of the Sound, and even took us under the water behind the falls.

This was followed by lunch where they announced we had a choice for our trip back: we could either be flown out, or return on the same bus we'd arrived on. Jim and I chose to stay with the bus as you had to pay extra to fly, and we were getting low on funds. There weren't a lot of people who picked this choice. I didn't mind though. There was a deep creek running alongside the road and the creek was full of flowers. It was beautiful. However, as we went through the hills the road was very narrow, barely able to take the width of two buses. We were going along very carefully when we came to a bend in the road, and met another bus coming around the bend, partly on our side. Our driver had nowhere to go. The best he could do was head for the creek while trying to keep the bus on the road. He managed to stop the bus, but it was hanging with the front lefthand wheel over the edge. Thankfully the bus was still upright. I don't know how the driver got out as the only way was to open the door and swing around it to the other side and hope someone was there to catch you before you fell down the side of the creek. He must have done something like that though, as he survived. It took a long time for the men to work it all out.

Our other holidays were not nearly so adventurous, though still full of good memories. Jim had always wanted to have a caravan holiday, and although that's not my liking, we decided to do that at Christmas time in 1970. We could only get a four-berth caravan and there were seven of us, but we decided to give it a go anyway. There were two single beds and the table folded down into a double bed. Stephanie and Lee-Ann slept top and tail in one bed, Meredith and Tim in the other, and Andrew slept in the pram placed in the doorway. Jim and I took the table-bed. The trip was around the west coast of the Eyre Peninsular—Venus Bay, Streaky Bay, Cleve, Elliston and then home again. At Elliston we had our first try at fishing—this was well before our holidays with Pat and Snow. Jim stayed at the caravan with Andrew while I took the other children fishing on the jetty, with nothing but a plastic reel of line and hooks. Surprisingly, we caught a little fish, but when we pulled it out of the water, the children saw it and started yelling: "Poor little thing, put it back Mum, put it back!" I'd never been fishing before and had no idea how to take the hook out of the fish, but somehow, I did it, and that was the end of our fishing adventure. We enjoyed our holiday but never tried caravanning again.

We kept the tradition of the annual holiday for many years, but as the kids got older they didn't always want to come. One year we had been invited to visit our cousin, Coral, who lived on Kangaroo Island. By this time, Lee-Ann and Andrew were getting older and didn't want to go for a holiday with Mum and Dad. Even so, we arranged to go, staying at their place in a caravan. It was a nice holiday, but the teenagers did a lot of growling and grumping, and I declared that this would be the last family holiday.

It was meant to be a reminder to the children to enjoy the opportunity, but as it turned out, I was right. This is the lesson I've realised as I've been writing this all down – life goes by in a flash, and it's best to savour every moment.

18

FAITH, FIRE AND FAMILY

Over the years, I found myself volunteering for just about everything that needed volunteers. Like Mum, I was already part of the Methodist Church Women's Fellowship and the CWA, but sometimes if something wasn't running, I would find like-minded townsfolk and we'd start it ourselves.

My sister-in-law, Yvonne was often my partner in crime. When our children were young we noticed there was no early learning centre for the children, so we decided we'd get a kindergarten going. We made enquiries at the Methodist Church as they had a good-sized Sunday school building, and they agreed to let us use it. When we put it to the mothers in the community, to see if it was something they'd like their children to attend, quite a few were keen.

We decided we'd start the morning with the children doing some singing and movement, and I played the piano. Audrey Albinus offered to help out, and Avis Clarke brought her son, so she stayed to help as well. That meant I could play the piano, Yvonne could sing the nursery rhymes and teach the actions, while Audrey and Avis helped supervise. We also set up a carpooling roster, to transport the children to and from the kindergarten. On one occasion I was taking the children home, and they were standing up in the back seat as we drove along. One young boy was standing behind me and rubbing his hand up and down my back.

"What are you doing?" I asked him.

"I've dropped my lizard down your back," he replied.

Yikes!

I leaned as far forward as I dared while we were in motion and said to him, "well find it, quick!"

And he did.

Rogue lizards aside, the kindy brought us a lot of fun. We held fancy dress parades where the children came in various costumes, and it often felt like a party. I also bought a very big teddy bear to help teach the children rules and manners —*look both ways before crossing the street*, and *always say please and thank-you*. The children enjoyed their kindy and we soon found that Booleroo people thought it a good idea, so they opened a kindy in the same way. All was going well until the government interfered with laws saying that any child-minding organisation must have trained teachers to run it. Thankfully, we weren't stopped so easily. The wife of one of the local farmers was a teacher, and she was prepared to take over the kindergarten. By this time Andrew was four years old, so I was happy to let her take it over, and it was good for Andrew to have someone other than his mother to conduct the kindy.

Eventually the government took over the running of the place, and the kindergarten was moved down to the school, and set up in the old teachers' living area. There was a special opening for the new venture and a plaque was placed on the wall, recording Yvonne and my part in getting it started.

Another group Yvonne and I participated in was the Mothers' and Babies' Health Association. This was a government-run organisation. They provided a clinic with trained nurses who visited the small towns fortnightly so the young women of the district could have their baby weighed and receive advice. This was a wonderful help for the young mums as many lived a long way from medical help, and sometimes a long way from their own family. In Melrose, the MBHA sister consulted in the local RSL room, along with Doctor Wheaton's clinics. There was a screen at the end of the room. The sister had a table and chairs and baby scales set up. Each mother took her turn with her baby to go behind the screen and consult with the sister, while the others waited sitting around the room. But the set up didn't allow for much privacy. Worse, Doctor Wheaton was usually consulting at the same time. Even though his consults were in the kitchen of the RSL building, his patients waited their turn in the same room as the MBHA clinic. Everything that was being said between the mother and the sister was heard, and often discussed, by those waiting to see the doctor.

I became a member of the MBHA after Stephanie was born, and soon after I attended the annual meeting with Yvonne. The club only had one meeting a year—possibly planned this way so it didn't take up too much time for the young mothers. However, both Yvonne and I thought they needed a club that would meet regularly, so it could support the work and the sister. We discussed it and decided that if we could win the vote at the annual meeting, Yvonne would take on President, I would be the Secretary, and together with members who wanted to see more outcomes, we could make the club active.

I turned to Mum immediately for advice. Mum had been a member and officer of the Country Women's Association for many years, so she was very familiar with ways to make things happen. She wrote down the order of the agenda and told Yvonne and I what to say and do. Armed with this information, we set off for the first meeting. And it worked—Yvonne was voted in as President, and me as Secretary.

It wasn't long and the club was booming. The members decided to hold their meetings at night so the husbands could babysit, thus giving them free rein at the meetings. We held meetings in each other's homes and made a program, having interesting speakers and activities. It wasn't long and the club agreed we needed a proper room for the clinic at the RSL rooms. We approached the RSL committee and asked if we could use the small room currently used for storage at the front of the building. The room had a big cupboard the height of the windowsill, which took up most of the space between the wall and the door. Even after everything belonging to the RSL was stored in the cupboard (instead of on the floor), the cupboard still had one section empty for our MBHA gear, and plenty of room to put things on top. We scheduled a working bee and painted the whole room a light blue, and bought some good quality floor covering. We hung white chintz curtains over the window, and when the table and client chair was put across the room, it left just enough space for the sister to get through to weigh the babies on top of the cupboard. Even though there was very little room to move, it made a comfy consulting room. And most importantly—it was private.

The MBHA eventually had a strong club and enjoyed the evening meetings, sharing recipes, sampling cooking, playing party games, and having dress up nights. It was their one night a month without the kids. But as the years went on, the older members resigned, and as younger women took their place, the meetings began to change. It's the usual thing that happens when the culture shifts, I suppose. Those who were older noticed that the young women didn't want to join in with the fun things we'd always found so entertaining, and the party games gave way to a glass of wine and a cigarette. As their children grew, the older women left, and the membership declined. Eventually, when new government rules came in and the sisters were no longer employed, the organisation was closed. It was a disappointment, after all the work Yvonne and I put in, and the years of community activities we'd enjoyed. But for everything there is a reason, even though we may not realise it. I can't help wondering if the reason here was to get us started on the road to Pentecost.

WHEN TIM WAS JUST A BABY, I used to take him to the MBHA sister each fortnight for his check-up. Imagine my surprise one day, instead of the usual visiting sister, I walked in for my appointment to find my old nursing matron, Lorna Catford. She had changed jobs and was now working for MBHA. She'd been appointed to do the Melrose-Wilmington run. I quickly found out that she had to find somewhere to have lunch after her Melrose appointments before she headed to Wilmington, so I invited her out to our place for lunch. It was so good to sit and chat with her, both to reminisce on old adventures from the Booleroo Hospital, but also because she was a woman who was well read and interested in everything. I arranged for her to come to lunch every fortnight, and it gave us plenty of time to discuss all manner of things.

One interesting development was Lorna had encountered a new expression of Christianity involving the baptism of the Holy Spirit. Recently, an old acquaintance from Booleroo had started to pastor a church in Pt Pirie. This pastor had been introduced to baptism of the Holy Spirit, including speaking in tongues, and he was telling anyone and everyone all about it. Lorna was a good Anglican and couldn't cope with it all, so she came to our home each fortnight with a new experience and a heap of questions about the whole subject. But the concept was new for Jim and me as well. We'd already heard of a group in Booleroo who were practising this 'Pentecostal Christianity' and everyone agreed they were quite crazy, claiming such things as people getting healed and such like. Then out of the blue, our local Methodist minister asked us if we'd like to go to Adelaide to hear a guest speaker at a church on the topic of the Holy Spirit. Jim couldn't go, but I went, and during the service I asked if they thought I could be healed from the heart condition I had.

God did heal me right there and then, but not of the heart condition—it was the migraine headaches I used to suffer, and to this day I've never had another one. I was quite changed after that experience. The Methodist Church of my upbringing was so subdued, and did not have any time for healing, speaking in tongues, or anything charismatic. But those things resonated deeply with me. Eventually, Jim and I decided to leave the Methodist Church, and we joined the 'crazy group' in Booleroo.

JOINING the Pentecostal church helped us grow in faith, and gave us more activities to be involved in, but of course my desire to volunteer in local community groups didn't stop.

I was still with St Johns, but it was taking up a lot of my time, and I was getting older. When the local Country Fire Service (CFS) decided to upgrade their communication set up, they asked for volunteers. The new communication radio, which broadcast from the top of the Mount, was operated from the CFS shed in Melrose. It had various radios in selected units belonging to farmers. In the event of a fire, someone would staff the radio at the CFS shed while maintaining contact with the farmers on the fire ground and the firefighting units, so everyone could be kept in contact. The men at the meeting decided to ask the ladies if they could help, so when Jim came home from that meeting, he asked if I'd be interested. All I'd have to do was staff the shed in the case of a fire, and test the farm units once a week. That seemed easy to me, so I said yes, and decided it was time to resign from St Johns.

This new position would be a much lighter load—or so I thought. I agreed that when it was my turn, I would go into the shed and sound the CFS siren, then call each farmer who had a unit, to test their signal. It didn't sound hard. However, I discovered that while other women had said they would be happy to help, they weren't able to come so regularly. It came down to Denise Davis and me. Still, we were prepared to rise to the challenge, even though we knew we'd have to figure things out as we went.

We turned up for our first lesson with Geoff Slee and Graham Blieschke, and they showed us how to use the microphone. Geoff held it firmly, straight in front of his mouth.

"Never hold it like this," he said. "If it's straight on like this, the person on the other end won't be able to understand what you're saying." Then he turned the mic to the side of his mouth. "When you speak have the mic turned to the side like this," he demonstrated.

"When you finish a conversation, you say 'out', not 'over and out' as they do in all the movies. 'Over' means: I've finished what I was saying but I expect a reply, while 'out' means: I've finished this conversation. Now you try," he said.

Denise and I did our little practice, as instructed, and Geoff said that was all we had to know. If there was a fire, we were to open the shed and stand by. He would always be at a fire, and would direct us as we went.

We were trained, ready to do our best when the time came. It all sounded very easy.

And then came our first fire. Both Denise and I got to the shed quickly, and set everything going, but when we contacted Geoff, we found he'd gone shopping to Pt Pirie. There we were, having to run the fire, and not knowing how. We did our best, but it wasn't long before we had chaos on our hands. Men were calling in and we were answering the call, but neither of us knew what to tell them, or what we were supposed to be doing. We just had to guess. This made the men angry, and finally one exploded, very rudely, making us both feel very small.

And then a voice came over the radio, quite patiently. "That will enough of that," he said.

It was one of the Wilmington CFS officers. And thankfully, he took over.

After our terrifying experience at the first fire, Denise and I got together and made a few rules. The place needed some organisation.

Every time the siren rang, there would be people coming in and out, crowding around, leaning over and getting in our way as we were trying to send messages. That made it very difficult, so we thought we'd make a screen at the side so people could look through the fly wire, but they couldn't get too close to the radio unit. That worked all right for a while, but it didn't keep people out for long. Finally, we got the men of the organisation to build us a small room at the back of the shed to use as a communications room—and we closed the door to keep everybody out.

The new little room was exactly what we needed. There were desks to work from. There was a window where people could get information without having to come into the room. There was another window for looking out over the Mount, and we could see what the men and the units were doing, right in front of us.

Now the system was more organised, we felt more comfortable asking other women to join as volunteers. I organised a roster, and each person spent one month coming in on Monday to test all the units in the farm vehicles, the main base unit at the shed, and also on top of the Mount. That worked well, as while each person had their turn, they were simultaneously being trained to do the job. It made a big difference when we had to attend a fire. Every year at the beginning of the fire season, we organised for everybody to get together to play out a fake fire, using cadets as well as other CFS members. We conducted the whole thing from the fire shed and the farmers' units wherever they were, but pretended that they were on the field.

Then came our first big fire. It started over on the other side of the range and spread into the Telowie Gorge, right over to the Wirrabara Forest.

Two of our CFS men were out on Survey Road watching this fire coming up from the other side of the hill. They were aware that if something wasn't done very soon, the fire would get away through the Woods and Forests fence, and into the Wirrabara Forest. They were reporting back to us at the shed, but it was as if they couldn't hear our replies. There was a complication. They had sent somebody from Adelaide to conduct the whole firefighting operation, and he was to run things from the Telowie base on the other side of the ranges. He was very rude, and considered we were a lot of country hicks who knew nothing. But we didn't realise the extent of it.

We had sent a couple of volunteers to take some food over to the Telowie base, and just as they approached the base, they heard our base calling their radio. But the officer didn't let anyone reply—he told his staff, "ignore that."

When she came back, she reported to me, and I then understood why our messages weren't getting through to our men up on the Survey Road—they were being stopped. However, because I now knew what was going on, I had my revenge. Our men were getting very tired, and they asked us to send more cigarettes with the next lot of food. The request was immediately followed by a message from Telowie: "Send some for us too."

But I chose to ignore that.

Well, that fire did exactly what the local CFS men feared it would do. It came right up to the Woods and Forest fence. Our men had wanted to open the fence and get in before the fire did, so they could do a backburn, but they were not allowed to, thanks to the stupidity of the Adelaide direction. The fire jumped over the fence and headed straight to the Wirrabara Forest. Fortunately, our men were ready for it, because they had been watching and waiting.

Everything went quite well with the fires after that. We learned how to do things quickly and efficiently, and our team was working well. Then the big one came, and we found there was a lot we hadn't learned.

19

THE MOUNTAIN AFLAME

On Thursday the 7th January 1988, the men were called out to a fire somewhere around the monument on Mount Remarkable. There'd been a dry thunderstorm, and a lightning strike had started a fire on the back slope of the Mount, near the old racecourse flat. It took the men two hours to reach it because the country was so inaccessible, but once they got there, they got the fire out, save for logs that continued to burn. The National Parks men were vigilant and patrolled the burning logs, but the treachery of that country in the hot, dry, windy weather, is unbelievable. On Saturday 9th January, all hell broke loose.

As soon as we heard the loud and long peel of the fire siren we knew there was trouble. Jim and my youngest son, Andrew, now a grown man, grabbed their CFS gear, and they drove to my daughter Lee-Ann's place to collect her husband, Simon. And off they went. When they reached the zone of the fire, they met the National Parks men coming out of the area, tired out and almost in tears because the fire had got away from them.

They had obviously been fighting hard. The CFS men went to the blaze, while we women swung into action at the communications base.

Feeling this could be a long fight, I began to make phone calls to personnel and prepared a roster to staff the base, but little did I know just how long it would be.

We had to call in as many men as possible. Units from all around the seeable district began calling in, as the smoke got thicker and higher.

As soon as I got the roster organised, I came home. We had arranged to have a birthday party for my granddaughter, so I rostered myself on for later in the night. Naomi's father, uncles and grandfather came home for the celebration too, but they were all so jumpy and wanted to get back to the fire, so they were gone before the party was finished.

I was due to go back on duty at about midnight. All this time, we'd had visitors—my cousin, Rod, and his family had been staying with us, but of course it was difficult for us to enjoy each other's company with the fire going on. They were due to leave at about 5am, so I would see them to say goodbye just as I'd be coming off duty. But two hours before my shift even started, I had a call from the communications room to say Jim was going to the top of the Mount. When I asked who was with him, the reply was, "just his crew," which was Simon and Andrew.

By now we could see the fire had a big front and it was coming up the back of the Mount, and quickly. Rod and his sons had been outside with the binoculars and could actually see the flames rising above the outline of the Mount above the Diocesan Centre. The horizon was an angry red against the black velvet of the night sky.

We had always been taught: if there is fire in the hills, never get above it, as fire goes quickly uphill. And I was hearing that my men were going to the top of the Mount, knowing the flames were almost there.

To my knowledge, Jim, Simon and Andrew were still out the back of the Mount, and they must have been headed on foot into the path of the fire. I couldn't rest, so I went back into the radio room to see what I could find out from there. But they couldn't tell me anything more.

Meanwhile the operations at the shed were expanding, and we had to move things around. The screen that divided the room to deaden the noise for the radio operators, was getting in the way, so we moved it out into the middle of the room. We started pinning the names of all the men on duty on it, as the board we usually used for this purpose was full.

Activity was intense in the room, and tension was growing. I'd been there a couple of hours or more when Jim came in. I was so relieved to see him, and when questioned, I discovered he'd gone up the fire track from Spring Creek with a Woods and Forests man, to see if they could tell how far up the front was. It was still dangerous, but less so than I had imagined. Andrew and Simon were still at the back of the Mount.

As the night wore on and the cooler night air moved in, things quieted down. But as Sunday dawned, everyone knew the battle to control the fire was lost. It was now a matter of getting in as much heavy equipment possible to push through breaks and stop it before it got out of the mountain area.

Dozers were called in from everywhere: Port Augusta, Port Pirie, E.&W.S., B.H.A.S. Local Earth Movers, and every farmer we knew who had one on their property. I knew it was wise for me to get Mum out of her cottage, so I got Margaret to take her to her home in Booleroo Centre. After some sleep on Sunday morning, I went back to the shed to find things had become a lot worse, and were right out of control. At about 11am, Carol was on radio duty, and had just heard that the fire was racing southward in an area that several men—including her husband Peter—were stationed. She was trembling, so I took over the radio while she left for a time.

Suddenly everything seemed to explode. The fire raced up the back of the hill just behind the town and poured over the top, and all the residents of old Melrose were evacuated. I sat at the radio watching the fire descend the front face of the Mount, about 400 yards in front of me. It seemed like a tidal wave of flame as each line of huge gum trees exploded into flames, leaping metres high and rolling still further down the side of the Mount.

Di Slee burst through the door, almost beside herself, saying, "I've had just ten minutes to decide what to take from the house!" I knew there were others in the same boat. The flames kept on coming towards me and the town, but I was so awestruck that I felt no fear. I remember thinking, "I wonder how long I must sit here before I should evacuate and leave my post." One of the young men from church appeared at the door, and I called out to him to ring the members of our church and tell them to pray. I'd called them before when I knew Jim was going up the Mount, and had been encouraged with the scripture, "The flame shall not be kindled against the Lord's people." I stood on that word now.

The flames intensified before my eyes. The change of shift came on, and I was relieved from the radio for a time, so I went outside the shed. I couldn't believe the almost deafening roar of the flames. Then suddenly, it was as if God had put out His hand and stopped the flames, saying "Thus far and no further." Although it was impossible, it looked as if the flames retreated up the hill, rolled off the end, and were gone, leaving burning trees in their wake.

All this time, there'd been a team of men working frantically around the line of the creek, from Laurie Bishop's to the monument, and they had set up a backburn. Of course, as soon as the two fires met, the raging inferno was beaten. It was an incredible sight.

While the battle was won on this front, the fire had beaten the fire fighters at the end of the Mount. It had gathered such intense heat and speed that it raced forward into the grasslands, and south along the range.

It was well into Sunday now. Different landowners had tried desperately to move their sheep but the hills are so steep, and mustering takes such a long time. One man managed to get his sheep to yards that had no undergrowth around it, but although that was the obvious place to put them, the poor animals were burned as the fire raced over them. Knowing they had no hope of holding it, the men turned to flee before the front and dropped back to a place where they hoped to be able to get a hold on it. Some of the men appeared unable to get out, so they drove over places they never thought they'd be able to go, to find safety from the flames. Others who had completed the backburn at the foot of the Mount now turned and headed for the Survey Road.

The fire had gone up behind Slee's and Davis's, crossed over Survey Road and was heading out through Schammel's and Bamman's, Crittendon's, Cameron's and down towards Murray Town—where Stephanie, my oldest, lived. She rang me while I was off duty and said she had packed the caravan and was going to Marg's at Booleroo Centre. I asked her to come back to our farmhouse at Gumville, and help me. I packed important papers, photos, clothes for a week and things I thought I couldn't replace. Lee-Ann did the same, and Marg came and did Mum's place. Everything went to Booleroo Centre, then the girls put the horse and all the sheep on the bean stubble, and we sent the dogs over to Booleroo. I had to stop then, knowing that I'd done everything I could. If we lost our homes, we'd just have to accept it.

Meanwhile the fire raced along the Survey Road with the teams of men just keeping in front enough to fight it at each house, and stopping any buildings from being destroyed. At Jillaby, even the trees right up to the house were burned. It seemed the devil himself was in this fire and couldn't be stopped, but the men did what they could, and were able to save the house.

The fire was burning westward as well, going over one hill after another. No one really knew which front to fight first. Back at the radio control room, things were a hive of activity. We had started with one VHF. radio, one standby radio, one CB radio and two telephones, but over the next hours things began to grow. The main radio lost signal at one point and although the radio operators had been trained to take certain action in these cases, the instructions were not followed. However someone had a spare radio on the back seat of his car, and that was installed immediately. It was proof that the CB radio was necessary, as we did not lose contact with the fireground at any time. Many women were now coming in and offering to help, including girls who had never worked there before. It became obvious that someone had to co-ordinate everyone in the radio room and so the job fell to me and Denise. We began working with the system of one being on while the other slept for as long as needed, and that worked well to start with. All other personnel were working four hours on, twelve hours off, but because of the relentless fight, the days and nights began to merge into each other. Soon, we really didn't know what day it was.

By now the section 52 (7) of the Act had been brought into force, putting the Regional Officer in charge of the fire. It was becoming clear that the supervisor needed relief as he'd been on duty for many hours, day and night, besides having his home threatened and land burned. A Command Centre was set up in the council chambers and two deputy supervisors were brought into action. These men, alternating duty, were placed in the communications centre, thus giving much-needed authority to make decisions for us. That was a great relief. By now, our operations had expanded to two VHF radios, one on channel 2 and one on channel 3; two CB radios, one on channel 20 and one on repeater 4 (being manned by WICEN), and three telephones. We were handling all incoming calls, plus all radio communications of personnel going into the fire and coming out, including the bombers and helicopters. The communication link between the fire fighters, the command centre and the outside world was vital. We were taking the knocks from those who were disgruntled. In a lot of cases I was doing that personally, trying to keep peace in a highly volatile situation in the case of both legitimate and imaginary complaints.

Now we had the Police in charge, coordinating the council personnel working to keep up with demands made in their area, Woods and Forests Supervisors, National Parks personnel, Radio repair men, and SES and CFS radio communication personnel from Adelaide.

Radio Operator (RO) 6, and later RO 2 were called in to help relieve RO 4.

The fire had grown to such an extent that it now had five different fronts, so it was divided into five sectors, each of which had a supervisor put in charge. Sector one from

Mambray Creek to Hancocks Look-out was controlled by National Parks. Sector two from Hancocks Look-out to the 'S' Bend at Terka was controlled by Wilmington CFS. Sector three from the 'S' Bend to Melrose started under a Melrose CFS officer—but when he came in to be the deputy supervisor at the communications room, Woods and Forests took over. Sector four was from Melrose to part way down the Bridle Track, with another Melrose officer in charge trying to oversee that sector plus act as deputy Supervisor. Sector five was from the Bridle Track to Mambray Creek.

All these people met twice each day to discuss how their sections were going and what moves had to be made to continue to combat the flames. I also attended the briefing meetings each day, which helped keep those of us staffing the radios in touch with what was being planned. The area from Melrose right around the burnt perimeter to the Bridle Track was now being patrolled by landowners, as that area had been brought under control. But the battle was far from over.

As the fire burned on down the western hills it came into the waterfall area, and the men found themselves in very steep and inaccessible country. Jim tells of being in an area where the heat was splitting off huge pieces of rock, which came hurtling down around them. To be hit could have meant injury or death. Andrew tells of one time when they had moved out on foot to the fire, and suddenly it came up around them. They retreated to the vehicle which was on burned ground, but still close enough for the flames to reach them. All of them tried to get into the cabin of the ute but they couldn't all fit, so Jim had to lay down in the back of the ute while the fire went over them. They tell how the smoke was choking and the heat almost unbearable. Jim said he thought he would cook. Another time Jim heard a crack and looked up to see a huge burning tree had broken off, falling down the slope towards him only to be snagged, luckily, on another tree that was jutting out. One firefighter spoke of dropping the men off at intervals along the creek bed and leaving them with ice-cream buckets to physically bucket the water from the creek, to try to put the fire out on the face of the cliff.

Meanwhile, in the communications shed, things were very tense. I was being stretched to my limit as I tried desperately to cope with everything that was going on and deal with the malcontents as well. I eventually managed to get off duty for my four hours, went home to bed only to find that my body refused to go on when the four hours were up. I rang the shed and spoke to Denise, asking if she could cope for a little longer. She said that was okay, and a little later she called back to tell me to stay where I was and get a proper rest. I was never so thankful for anything, and I slept for quite a few hours.

It made all the difference. When I returned to the shed, I found that the chief inspector from the Pt. Pirie police, who was also in charge of the disaster plan for the district—and this sure was a disaster now—had been called in. With a fresh eye he'd summed things up and rearranged everything. Communications had spilled out of our room and had taken over the whole shed. Placing a table across the big sliding door area for the personnel registration, we made an area under the window for one CB and one phone, which I oversaw, while the rest stayed in the room. Two other women had been brought in to help volunteer in my area, thus giving each of us a chance to have a reasonable time off to sleep. Some of the women had property being burned or threatened, and almost all of us had men out fighting. Because of this, some of the ladies were reluctant to leave their post when relieved. In a couple of cases I had to order them to go. It wasn't easy, but with the extra rest I was able to deal better with the high emotions.

The fire was now at the top and over the Mount, from the show grounds to the Diocesan Centre and further down. Knowing I would be the only one at home during my time off, I chose instead to go to Lee-Ann and Simon's, as Simon's parents, were there, so I'd be able to get some sleep without worrying. Soon I went back to work, but things, although tense and pressured, were becoming almost routine now.

Andrew, Simon and Jim headed out along Sector Three, as that was the next section being threatened. The men in this sector were preparing to do a backburn, as the fire was coming down the Mount quickly now. I was feeling nervous. This would be the time that would tell if we could control it, or if it would get away on the plains and reach our home. Simon's father had kindly gone to our home and set up a sprinkler system. Still, the fire kept coming. I wasn't surprised when the woman who lived just down the creek from me, rang to say she wasn't coming back in for duty as the fire was coming that way. "Okay," I replied. "I'll organise it."

"But Jenny," she said. "What about you?"

"I've evacuated all I can take and if the rest goes, it goes," I said, knowing it was the only way I could afford to look at it. By the time evening was approaching, I was due off. The backburning had started so I went home. I knew our neighbours, the Moultons, were still at their house. As they were between me and the fire, I rang and told them I was on my own and asked them if anything happened, to let me know. With that, I laid down in the study by the CB, with the air conditioner on. The heat in these three or four days had been oppressive, keeping in the high 30º C and low 40º C. I figured the air conditioning would help me sleep and the CB would warn me if anything went wrong. I only slept in fits and starts and could hear the radio chatter—the men along the Wilmington Road needed someone to relay for them. Sometimes I couldn't help myself, and I did some relaying myself. I heard Jim, Andrew and Simon on the CB at different times, and I felt relieved to know where they were and that they were okay. Then, just before I was due to go back to work, there was a call from a group by the Diocesan Centre track asking for a chainsaw. I took a little walk outside and found our chainsaw, then phoned Denise and told her I'd take it to the men. Jim almost had a fit when he found out. "We've lost our chainsaw now," he said. But he was wrong because it turned up later.

The men backburned right along a new bulldozed firebreak up behind the houses at the foot of the Mount and managed to stop the fire's advance across the plain. This backburning continued during the day but the fire kept creeping down the Mount and further north. Besides this, all the country west of the Survey Road was burning out of control. A backburn was being set up west of Waterman's place. Trying to control all areas and have everything running smoothly and to time became difficult. While one operation should start in one place it would be held up because personnel or equipment were needed unexpectedly elsewhere. On one occasion everyone was concerned as the northern backburn fanned by a strong north-westerly wind raced along behind the Diocesan Centre, but then there was a change in the wind to a south-westerly, and it was stopped.

By now everyone was jumpy and worried about spot fires. We began to call on anyone we could think of to help watch out for us. There were smouldering trees everywhere, standing like glowing sentinels, spitting out showers of sparks. The fire still burning down the western slopes had reached Baroota, and a bit further on it caused Highway One to be closed. Units were arriving from everywhere as our own local men were asked to do the impossible. Even units from the Adelaide Hills were called in, and a bus load of men from Port Lincoln arrived to help with the fight. Still the hungry flames were not satisfied. With encouragement from its friend the wind, the fire jumped the backburns at Spring Creek where the men had been working feverishly to stop it. And off it went towards Wilmington. It raced towards the main road and once again it seemed no one was going to beat it. After it burned over the main road at Terka, it was stopped from spreading eastward. But it still raced on north.

Then we had a radio call to say Jim was coming in, in a hurry, with Simon, who had been stung on the head by bees. I notified St Johns and went back to the radio room, only to get the message that several more men were coming in with bee stings. One of the bee owners had decided to move his bees out of the area without them being locked in properly. They were maddened with fear by the smoke, so look out anyone in sight.

Soon Wilmington was thrown into a panic as the fire approached. Wilmington base was in full swing now. The townsfolk had evacuated to the school swimming pool area, and the residents of the senior citizens home were taken to Booleroo Centre Hospital. The fire had burned fiercely through the Alligator Gorge, right over the battery which seemed not so long ago to have been burnt. The men fought well and were able to stop it in the bare paddocks on Fricks Road. There was a track pushed around through to Hancocks Lookout, towards Mambray Creek. As the pressure was relieved, the landowners in each area took over the patrolling, watching all the burning trees carefully, but also taking a lot of men out of the fighting force on the front. During early hours of Thursday, a very strong wind blew up and caused a further outbreak at Wilmington. The people once again evacuated their homes, but once again the flames were stopped, although it seemed that the Alligator Gorge and north area were still going strong.

But this time fate was on our side. As the fire burned towards the breaks and backburns, with the help of the helicopter's reconnaissance and the bombers, the flames became contained.

Friday 15th January dawned much cooler, and at last the monster fire was declared contained. On Saturday 16th January it was announced that the fire was under control.

God be praised. More than 35,000 hectares were burnt, 400km of fencing valued at $800,000 destroyed, and something like three to five thousand sheep lost. But no human lives were lost, no homes destroyed, nor any major injuries. The trees burned on for months, and the trauma affected the people for a long time to follow. But as with all things, all would eventually be repaired.

Water bombers on standby - January 1988

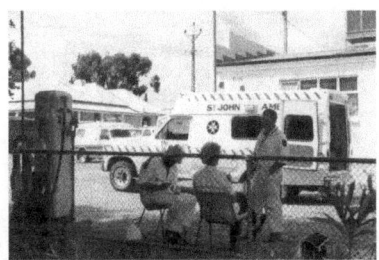

St Johns on standby - 1988 bushfire

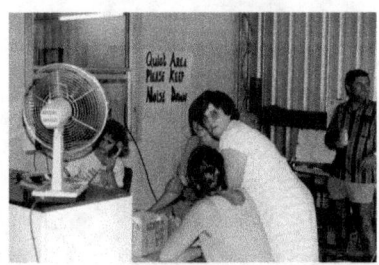

Extended radio room - 1988

20

MUSIC TO MY EARS

Over the years, so many of the community events that had made our town thrive, gradually wound down and then disappeared. One of these was the cherished movie night.

This staple of my childhood and young adult life, had gone from old silent movies requiring a pianist to play the accompanying music based on prompts like "romance" or "water, to movie nights that came with sound as 'talkies' became popular, and later, the local drive-in at Gladstone where a giant screen was set up in a big open area with a canteen in the middle and listening posts all over. Each carload of people drove in after paying at the gate, and then picked the best position. The speaker from the post hooked on the window of the car. After getting our popcorn or goodies from the canteen, we were ready to sit back in our cars and enjoy the movie. It was a different atmosphere to movie nights in the town halls, but still, it was an outing where the community came together. But as time went on the inevitable happened: the drive-ins closed as TV became the thing, and everyone stayed home.

Many of us missed these sorts of community gatherings. From time-to-time people would suggest restarting some of the by-gone activities, and one suggestion was to hold a movie night. There was a couple from Peterborough who had all the equipment, and they were trying to get movie nights going again in local towns. We decided to organise one in Melrose. It was a lot of work but we thought it was worth the trouble. There was a good response. Several people suggested we hold these nights on a regular basis. As there seemed to be the support, we put the idea into action and soon were holding movie nights fortnightly. It meant those of us who were involved had to be at the hall early where we dragged the chairs out from storage, got carpets and put them down the front for kids to sit on, and set up stalls for the snacks. I was responsible for making honeyed popcorn and we had other confectionary to sell. The movies went along well for a while and then we noticed, just as we had found for other ventures, they began to drop off. But worse than that, we noticed people were bringing their children, settling them in, and then going off to the pub for the evening, leaving us to babysit the children. The situation was not good—our takings were down, and we didn't need the responsibility of other people's young ones, and so the whole thing eventually folded.

But I was determined to keep the music going, somehow.

Just as Mum had done with me, I made sure that as my children grew, they were all taught to sing songs and join in with the music. When we went on long trips, we passed the time with singing games. The children would think of a word or subject, and I'd have to sing a song about it. There were many car rides where we would start singing. Jim would drive and listen as the rest of us sang at full voice, a couple of the children even learning to harmonise.

We were also lucky to have a pianola which Ella had left for us. It presented an opportunity I couldn't miss. I made arrangements to have piano lessons with Vera Fuller, the local piano teacher. I learned to read the music without any trouble but couldn't read it quickly enough to play it. I tried my best anyway.

I'd always wanted to play a guitar so I could sing my hillbilly songs, but Jim wouldn't have any of that. Then one day he agreed that if I could get a guitar for a certain (impossible) price, I could get one for my birthday. Thankfully, my sister, Marg, came across a very cheap guitar at Port Augusta. She told the shop assistant how much I wanted one, and he discounted it for her. My dear old guitar. It didn't have any extras such as a case, but Mum got busy and knitted me a guitar case with leftover bright yellow yarn. Over the years I've had all parts of it get broken but Jim put screws or glue around it, and it just kept on going. He even replaced one of the tuning knobs with a washer soldered on in its place.

I took to the guitar quickly but still struggled with the piano. Once Meredith observed I was still struggling to read the sheet music. "Mum," she said, "why don't you play the chords on the piano? You know what they are, you've learnt them all for the guitar."

And she was right. Thinking of it this way made all the difference. The melody of the songs was hidden in the chords. From then on I was able to play the piano at church, as well as at home.

I also started teaching the guitar. Soon I was approached by a man from Peterborough to ask if I'd consider teaching the children for a TAFE course. I had to have ten students, and it would be some good extra income. I thought I'd give it a go, and I started lessons at Orroroo School. It didn't take me long to realise it was a disaster. I had ten children, some musically orientated, some who would like to be, and some who couldn't care less. And I had to try to teach them the same thing at the same time. I struggled through the first term but I was soon onto my boss to try to straighten it all out.

"Some of the children have learned a bit of piano and can read the music, but others don't have a clue," I explained.

My boss told me they didn't particularly want the children to be able to read music.

"What!" I exclaimed. "How can you learn an instrument without learning to read music?"

Anyway, I put it to him that I was happy to take each child for a half hour each if they'd let me. The answer was that I could, but I would only be paid as if they were all together. So I made arrangements with the parents and had them come to my home for their lessons. It worked very well. Of course I didn't get the pay I should have, but it was worth it to give the children a proper go. I kept teaching until Andrew was about seven, and at that point I realised I needed to be free after school to attend to my own children, so I gave it away.

But I didn't give up the guitar. My neighbour, Jan, and I were taking singing lessons from Mr Wild, and we found it was useful to sing together for practice. From this, we started a little entertainment group and called ourselves The Gay Jays. We sang anywhere we were asked. Then I began adding some of my students, so we changed our name to the Alphabets. My children were also involved. Both Stephanie and Meredith played their guitars and Tim had a little set of drums to provide some rhythm. There were other members from time to time. We were invited to sing at Senior Citizens homes, and hospitals, and for any functions held at the halls. Once, we went to Port Pirie Hospital to sing for the oldies there. They had gathered them all together in the room and we came in, happily presenting our program. One poor old lady was in the middle of the group but could not sit up, so she had an over-way table in front of her with a pillow on it. She seemed to be beating time along with us, when suddenly she called out, "tell them to shut up!" That was a bit of a rude shock.

When Andrew was at high school, I discovered the reason I couldn't read music quickly enough. Andrew was struggling with school and eventually he received a diagnosis of dyslexia. That problem hadn't been recognised in the schools before. When we had a teacher from America come to our school, it was a big eye opener for us. I had to do a lot of work with Andrew to get him through his education, but soon, I realised he wasn't the only one with dyslexia. I was learning a lot about myself as well.

One day I was chatting to Jan about my problem reading music. I asked her how she managed to look at both the bass and treble staves at the same time. Jan told me she could see them both at once. When she said that, I made the connection. I only had a sight span of about two centimetres before I had to move my eyes. Other people didn't have to move their eyes at all and could take in whole sections. Once I knew what the problem was, I didn't get so frustrated with myself. Instead, I just focused on playing chords.

Because of my love of music, I was pleased when a new group formed in Booleroo Centre, known as the Patchwork Players. These people loved getting together to perform different plays. I wasn't involved to start with, but when they decided to produce *Oliver*, they needed a lot of children as extras, so Lee-Ann and Andrew took part. That got me interested and so I joined. We had so much fun putting things together. As he got older, Andrew got involved with the lighting and sound, and as a family we all joined in where we could. I wasn't up front singing, but I would assist the producer. It was a time of much fun. We performed *Show Boat*, *Fiddler on the Roof*, and *South Pacific*. *Annie* was a production I'd decided to sit out for, but right before the show, the lighting person pulled out. Andrew was in charge of all backstage production, and he didn't know what to do. So, mother to the rescue, I said I'd do it.

We sat down at the kitchen table with a lighting desk drawn on a piece of paper. Andrew had the script and list of things that had to be done, and I began practising on the drawing. The first thing I had to do was to make sure the master switch was off, then if I made any mistakes behind the curtain, no one out front of house would know. I practiced as much as I could and went to the theatre that night, confident it would be all right because Andrew was managing everything. The first night was a success. The next night I had more confidence. Andrew was directing us from behind the curtains, and we listened through our headphones for his directions. About halfway through the second night, I was preparing for the next scene's lighting when I heard Andrew yelling through the headphones.

"Mum! What are you doing?"

I was thrown into a panic. What was wrong? I looked around the lighting board in horror. Then it hit me. I had forgotten to turn the master switch off. I threw it off immediately and thankfully it hadn't made a lot of difference, but it could have been a disaster. It was at that moment I decided lighting wasn't for me.

While we were having fun with the plays, Kathy, one of the local teachers, came up with the idea of performing a

Cantata. This was something I'd never done before, so I turned up to audition. There were plenty of people who wanted to join in, and Kathy soon had a group of singers. The first show she chose was *The Glory of Christmas*. This was a new and exciting experience, telling the story using only singing. There was a choir, soloists, and smaller ensembles, each adding their bit to the story. Tim and Andrew joined another male singer to make up a group of shepherds. I sang a duet with a male soloist. The Cantata was well received and it wasn't long before people were asking us to do another one. We did several during the next few years, but slowly singers left the group, and new ones were not around.

The last big event I got involved with was the celebrations for the 150th Jubilee of South Australia, with the 200th celebration of the landing of Captain Cook's First Fleet in Australia. The Patchwork Players decided that, as it was an important occasion, the club should do something special. They had a good bank account at the time, so they were able to get scripts for *Old Time Music Hall*, which performed for the 1986 South Australian Jubilee, and *My Fair Lady* for the 1988 celebration. Moira McKay was the producer for *Old Time Music Hall*, and she had a plan which she presented to the club and we loved it, so work started immediately. There was not a lot of time to put it together. And then the disaster struck. Moira sent a message to the meeting to say she'd come down with rheumatic fever and had to pull out leaving us with no producer-director for our show.

After a lengthy discussion, it was decided to ask me if I would take on the role. Why me? I thought about it, but it would have to be different, as I couldn't do someone else's plan. They agreed, so I worked out a way forward. I tried to accommodate everything Moira had told me about her vision—the bits and pieces I'd heard, anyway. We used the Booleroo Hall and the CWA rooms for our rehearsals, as we needed several groups practicing at once. We recruited as many people as possible to perform, even several older folks joined. There were soloists and elocutionists, gymnasts, comedians, plus small singing groups and short plays. Each group were given an area to practise and I circulated around making sure they were happy and had all they needed. Everyone was working at top rate and doing an excellent job. I was so pleased with them all. But as I went from group to group, I started getting comments.

"You poor thing, the strain of all this must be terrible."

"How are you managing all of this, I hope it doesn't get you down."

"It's a wonder you can sleep at night with all this pressure. Are you all right?"

I thought this was odd. From my perspective it was going well—was I missing something? I concluded I wasn't missing anything. Everyone was doing exactly what I asked of them, and it worked. When the program was presented there was a strong positive response. Though the show was two hours long and very tiring, everyone felt it was a job well done.

Music has played such a big part in my life, and so it was hard for me when I realised that there was some damage to my throat. I don't know what happened, but I began to find I couldn't reach the higher notes. As time went on things got worse. I could still sing but I couldn't manage it for long, and the muscles in my throat seem to get weaker and weaker. I hardly ever sing these days unless I have to, and that doesn't improve things. The music of everyday is no longer a pleasure for me to listen to, and so I don't sing around the house anymore. I find that now the piano has been replaced with electronics, all we get is loud noise. But I raised my children and grandchildren on musicals, whether that be live or watching the classics on old videos. I hope they will pass it on. I hope that no matter how technology and society continues to change, we will keep coming together to sing, perform and share stories.

That is community.

21

NEW FAMILIES

Children grow up so quickly. The time of boyfriends and girlfriends and engagements brought a whole new set of learning experiences. When Meredith was nineteen, she became engaged to an Italian boy named Nick, who she met at Bible College. While we were pleased to welcome Nick to the family, we had some interesting cultural clashes to work through. Nick's mother was a very particular woman—a strict evangelical Christian with a strong code of what should and shouldn't be done. She was very opposed to jewellery, so there was no engagement ring to flash around. If the young couple wanted to show everyone the ring, it had to be done without her knowing anything about it.

We got around the problems as best we could. We decided to give them an engagement party at Melrose with all of our family and friends. But none who were on Nick's list—that list was reserved for every Italian in the neighbourhood, some of whom Nick didn't even know—were able to drive the three and a half hours up to our town. But we celebrated in our own country way. We set a date for the party.

Stephanie was thinking of coming back to live at Melrose, decided to bring our car and a lot of her things home that weekend. Everything was being prepared for the engagement when suddenly the phone rang. I answered it and was greeted by tears and those scary words: "I had an accident."

It had been raining which made the road slippery, and when she got to Stone Hut, there was an oil slick on the road from the cars going around that corner. The car had slipped to the side and down the road, to the rails at the crossing, and there it hit. Stephanie found herself in the car and unable to move. Eventually she got out and ran up to the first house along the line, and rang the bell. When the man came to the door, he told us later, he thought she was drunk, but soon found she was shocked and in tears. This all meant I had to hand over the engagement arrangements to Mum and Margaret, while Jim and I went to Stone Hut to get Stephanie and then rush back for the party.

All went well, and thankfully, Stephanie was fine.

She recovered from the shock, and decided to try to find work at Melrose as she thought things would be better for her near home as she was pregnant and could use extra family help. Stephanie approached Jim's cousins, who owned the shop at the time, to see if she could rent the two roomed premises that had been closed off from the main shop to make into a hairdressing salon. They readily agreed.

"That will be good for my business," they said to me. "People will go to Stephanie to get their hair done and then come into the shop and buy."

The room was quickly converted to a salon and it wasn't long before it was in full swing. And then in November, along came baby Isaac, a couple of weeks early. I had the joy and privilege of babysitting while his mum was working. The first words he must have learned would have been, "the baby is awake." ... "Alright I'll be there as soon as I have this next hairdo finished."

The dear little mite spent hours sucking a finger on Granny's shoulder while he waited.

All the family seemed to be coming back to Melrose at this time. Tim was offered a job at Fountain Centre Christian School and so after spending some time in Adelaide trying for a job and getting nowhere, he came back. Lee-Ann's husband Simon also got a job at the school and the two of them took a house in Booleroo. It was wonderful having the family at home. During this time we suffered another drought and had to get rid of all our sheep. Jim had to shoot 200 of them, and they were buried in the erosion out at Puckridges. It was a difficult time, and I was grateful to have the children home.

One of the things we got involved with was the "Miss South Australia" contest which raised money for the Spastic Centre, now Cerebral Palsy Alliance. The previous year's winner of Miss South Australia had judged the Miss Show Girl competition at the Melrose Show. Meredith won the competition, and as a result was asked to be the representative for our area. I sat down and made a list of all the best workers we could ask to make up a committee, and they readily agreed to join. We decided to call the representative for our region, "Miss Mt Remarkable", and we then made a list of all the fundraisers we would do. When it came to the end of the Miss South Australia competition, everyone went to the Festival Theatre to watch the judging. We were amazed at how many flowers were sent to the girls that were entrants. They had rooms full. Meredith had some but nothing like the others had. And then the delivery boy came to her door with a beautiful container with one red rose in it. It was from Nick. I seem to recall that the other girls were jealous of the one red rose which had so much more significance than the huge floral arrangements that were everywhere.

In the end, Meredith didn't win the competition. but it was a wonderful experience.

22

THE COUNTRY WOMEN'S ASSOCIATION

As I got older, in so many ways I found myself following in the footsteps of my Mum; whether that be certain ways of housekeeping, getting involved in community activities, or my love for all things music. Another way I followed in her footsteps was my involvement with the Country Women's Association. Ever since I was a child, the CWA was part of my life. During the war, I was with Mum at all the comforts fund meetings. Then when we were at Delamere and I did correspondence school from home, I went with her to meetings. I wasn't able to join the organisation as a child, but because I was there, I was allowed to join in with anything that was taking place. I got to go to cooking demonstrations, and hear speakers on all kinds of subjects, learn handicrafts, and on special occasions dressed up in costumes from other countries. Mum dressed me up as a young lady from Wales. Because I was always with Mum in this way, it followed that when I turned sixteen, I would finally join. I already felt like a member, but sixteen is the youngest a member could be. I was a member of the Wilmington branch and went along with Mum to all the meetings. When I was married, I transferred to the Melrose branch, but the branch there dropped off for a number of years, as did my participation when I was so busy in my new life as a wife and mother. But I remember when Carolyn was stillborn, my room became a beautiful garden of flowers that were sent to me in my sorrow from the women of the Wilmington CWA.

Mum was the sort who readily took office at any time, but only at branch level. There were levels you could be involved—branch, group, divisional and state. As I had so much training from Mum, it seemed logical for me to take office as well, and once the children had grown up, I was free to get involved. Then came my foray into political life, while I made CWA my main interest. One of the best things about the CWA was the rule that you could only hold office for three years, then you had to relinquish that position, but could take another one. I did several turns as branch president, and then I took office as group president. Holding offices helped me to grow, and it was also a lot of fun. Every year we studied a different country and had a group meeting with entertainment to celebrate that country. One year, the entertainment was that each group had to come with someone representing a country. The costumes were very well thought out. I'd arranged for Mum to be the judge, and she came dressed as Queen Elizabeth the Queen Mother. She looked just like her as she went to each of the entrants and shook hands with them.

When my three years was up as group president, I stood for divisional president. The division covered quite a large area and had twenty-four branches. It was my job to visit each group once a year if possible, and I was the link between the state, and the groups and their members. If, for instance, there was an accident, say someone's house was burned down, I would be contacted and then I would find out the details of what we could do to help. Then I got the information to the state. They would arrange for the people concerned to go and buy what they needed, and the state would organise with the store to pay for it.

There were several other duties I had, but I always thought the emergency services was an important one. One place I wanted to visit was Yunta as it was the northern-most branch in the division, and it was rare that anyone got there. I made arrangements to visit them, taking our group president with me. It was such an unusual meeting. When we arrived, the members were all there to greet us with morning tea, and I started with a short morning talk. As time moved on a few of the ladies stood, packed up, and left. I thought that was a bit rude, but shortly two or three new ladies arrived, quickly sat down and joined in. As we headed to midday, some of the ladies went out and prepared lunch, and we were enjoying a meal together when suddenly two or three other ladies left. Then, just as we started the afternoon session, there was another lot of ladies arrive. They all stayed for the rest of the time, but I was fascinated at the way everyone just came and went with nothing said.

"Oh, that's normal," one of the ladies explained. "They work on the stations around, and some come from a long way and can't spare the time to stay, but they do their best."

That definitely changed my view. I was suddenly grateful to these girls who would go to so much trouble to come to a meeting.

The next step was to do work at state level. At first, I joined the Social Issues Fact Finding Team, a group of women who met on a monthly basis to discuss and act upon various problems that had been brought from the members or branches. Each member of the SIFFT team had a portfolio which they shared with one or two other members. Their job was to research and respond to the problem each month, meeting with the whole team to report. My portfolio was Media and Politics. I worked on that team for about eleven years. At the same time, I was holding office at state level in the role of State Property Officer.

At that point I had said to Jim, "Let me go for State President, and then I'll resign and we'll find something we both like doing." But that didn't happen because one of the rules of the CWA is that the State President may not be the wife of any politician or clergyman. Jim had just been ordained as the local pastor of the CRC, and I had to resign. But not to worry, I soon found a new group to join—the Melrose Districts History Society.

During my time as a state officer, I gained a lot of experience. This was when computers were coming into general use, and the State Office thought we should give as much help as possible to the members who wanted to learn. We only had one member on the State Executive who knew anything about computers, other than me. Betty was a city member so she was given the job of setting it all up. I had been working with computers for a few years, since I worked in the school library. I was taught by James Nickel from America. This was back in the old days before the Windows program. I got all my set up from a firm in Adelaide that you joined, and then you were part of that family. Betty got all her information from the various businesses in the city that were trying to sell computers—the sort that when you bought one you didn't see them again. Still, we were able to pool our knowledge, and eventually it was agreed we would run some classes for the members. I was to provide classes for my division. It was great fun. The classes were held on weekends over two days, and usually held in a school where the computers were supplied. I would start the day by giving a talk about all the parts of the computer and what they were for. I had some hardware for show and tell, the inside of the computer which I got from Andrew. Then we would have a go at typing letters to get a feel for it. This would be followed by playing a game of Patience. Then, starting to write a letter. The oldest pupil I had was ninety. I don't think she got past Patience.

Another thing I learned was how important it is to present yourself properly if you are doing public speaking. We were schooled on how to dress and advised that you should not have anything that looks out of place, as it takes the attention away from your subject. This was brought home to me when I was speaking at a meeting at Ororoo. I'd had a bad morning and everything seemed to be going wrong, but I eventually got away to the meeting thinking, *I must hurry or I'll be late.* I was more than halfway to the venue when I glanced down and saw I was still wearing my shoes from the cow shed. But I couldn't go back. Oh dear, what to do? I had a CB in the car, so I called another lady to see if she could go past our place and get my good shoes. Thankfully she was able to, although it would make her late. However, she kindly came to the rescue and managed to work it into the morning talk on presentation. She made a big thing about the fact that I had not taken any care about my shoes and had come to the meeting with dirty and shabby shoes. The ladies were horrified when my appearance was pointed out to them publicly, but everything was put to right when I was presented with my good shoes and the point had been made. I was able to change my shoes and it seemed like it had been planned.

Probably the most embarrassing thing that happened to

me while in office was at the State Conference which was held in the Adelaide Town Hall. The auditorium is always full for the conference and there are always several dignitaries attending. They sit in a row onstage with the State President—usually the Governor or his wife, the Mayor of Adelaide, and two or three others. Others who are set to take part in the proceedings sit at the back of the stage. On this occasion I had to respond to a proposition that was to be presented, so I took my place on the stage in the back line. All was going well when my notes slipped off my knee. I bent to pick them up and, *swish*, my chair slipped out from under me and I went down with a mighty thump, right in the middle of someone's proposal. I felt the eyes of three or four hundred people, and a row of very surprised dignitaries turned, wondering if they were being attacked. I was very embarrassed when I eventually came to the mic to do my piece.

I had my one and only visit to the casino when I was on the SIFFT Team. It was during the drought of the 1990s, and I had to go to Parliament House to speak to some politicians about the way the drought relief money was being handled. The state president came with me to this appointment, but we were there early, so she asked if I had ever been to the casino. I'd never had the pleasure, so she suggested we go in while we were waiting. We didn't go very far but it was interesting to see it. After that we attended the appointment with a couple of politicians who we were lobbying to get a fairer deal for the farmers. Drought and debt were ever-present issues facing the members of the CWA. Jim and I weren't immune. I remember in the 1970s we were reduced to selling most of our stock, and we only had the nucleus of our cattle left. The cows were being sold for as little as twenty cents although ours went for two dollars, which is a great loss as we paid up to $150 for them. Then in the 1980s, the drought was a killer—we had no choice but to shoot some of our sheep, which was heartbreaking. Everyone was doing it tough. People were being forced off their land and some had even taken their own life.

One situation that had been brought to SIFFT was a family overcome with debt and having taken a huge loan from the government. The man had reached the end, and taken his life. This left the wife with three little children, having to manage the debt. Now the government had given her a short time to return the loan as it had been given to her husband, not to her. What was worse back then, was that suicide was not talked about. It was all hushed up. So the CWA were right in there, fighting her case.

After I had done my bit in the state arena, I came home with the intention of just being a local branch member again. But things were becoming difficult in Melrose. Young people were leaving the district and we couldn't get new members. Finally we decided to close the local branch and join Wilmington. Even so, there were only three of us left to join. Still, I had done a full circle, and I received my fifty years of service badge at a dinner at the Wilmington Hotel.

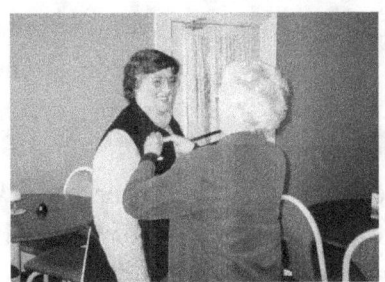

Receiving the 50 years of service badge

It was then that I resigned from the organisation, because

Mum, Grandma Hamlyn as she was known by my children, needed me.

Mum had moved to Mt. View Homes when she was eighty-nine. It had been her choice to make the move. Jim and I were away and, as she was worried about being left alone on the farm, so we suggested she go to the homes for respite care. She agreed, though made it clear she had no intention of staying.

When we came to pick her up, we asked if she enjoyed her time there.

"Yes," she said. "So much so that I've booked myself a room to move in."

Time went on and Mum was still in good health when she reached the age of 100, and received her letter of congratulations from the Queen. But soon her mind started slipping. She couldn't remember what year it was, and sometimes thought I was her mother. She also started becoming very distressed in the evenings, so I started to visit every day to help her settle. But she was deteriorating more and more.

I was having my own health problems at this time. I came down with some nasty virus in the bowel on the Sunday before Christmas, and so I landed in hospital—yet again, it seemed. At that point in my life, I felt I was keeping the hospital in business. Two days of drip, and another of drinking a strange South African concoction, then a day of rest, and I came home on Friday, just in time to miss the town Christmas in the Park.

By this time, Mum was hardly ever awake when I went to see her, so we cancelled the arrangements to have Christmas midday meal with her—I could see it might well be Jim and I, sitting in her room eating while she slept. Instead, we visited her in the morning, and I was pleased to see she was awake. We chatted a little, delivered a kiss that Tim and sent, and gave her a Christmas hug. She didn't want to talk for long because she said she could not get her breath.

"I just can't get the air in somehow," she said.

As we left, I cried again, as I had been doing every time I visited her, and I said to Jim that her heart was failing. I recognised the symptoms.

But it was Christmas, and we had to carry on. We went home and entertained a young couple, who were having multiple struggles with their own families. We had them over for the midday meal and it was quite festive. I felt they really enjoyed it. Then we set off for Adelaide to stay with my daughter Lee-Ann, who had been living there many years now. Christmas dinner was at my son Andrew's house, with his wife Tonya, her parents, and Lee-Ann, Simon and their children. The next morning, we had a larger Bishop family gathering at Lee-Ann and Simon's house. The little kids had got a swimming pool for Christmas, and we had a great day doing nothing but eating and watching the kids at play, and having the odd doze.

We stayed in the city on the 27th as well, so Simon and Lee-Ann could go out with friends and we could look after the children. It was while I was hanging out some washing that I received the phone call from the Mt View Homes to say that Mum had passed away peacefully in her sleep.

Of course I cried again, and did for a long time after. Meredith and her husband Nick came around straight away, and we began the difficult task of letting people know. When Simon and Lee-Ann got home, I was so grateful for Simon's reaction. He immediately got out the crystal glasses and some non-alcoholic wine to drink a toast to Mum's long and fruitful life. She had reached 103. He then began to imagine the people she would have met who'd have gone before, and it encouraged me so much.

We came home on the Wednesday and started making arrangements for the funeral. It was fortunate that two of Don and Von's family were over from Sydney, and were able to come. The day was a stinker, 44°C in the shade, but the funeral director was very good. During the funeral, Amy, Mum's oldest great grand-daughter, read the eulogy—which was quite long, to fit in 103 years of activity. Mum's favourite old song, "In the Garden of My Heart", was played on video. Jim gave the message, and reminded us all of Mum's faith in the Lord Jesus Christ. Mum had requested a private funeral, so when we went to the cemetery, only the family came. The funeral director allowed us to have the short service in the shade of the gum trees, and we said our last goodbyes there.

And so, it was a sad ending to the year. But we looked forward to the birth of two new grandchildren in the year ahead, and we hoped that, as with all those we had lost, their memories would live on and their traditions and habits would gain new life in the children to come.

Jennette with Alice on her 100th birthday

23

VISITORS

You would think that once my five children grew up, left home and started families of their own, that our big old farm house would feel empty.

But that has never been the case.

I've been very fortunate to have regular visits from the grandchildren, some of whom were living in the city so would come and stay for weeks at a time, getting to experience farm life.

But we have had far more visitors than just family. This was because Jim had a terrible habit of inviting anyone and everyone around for a meal and a chat, whether he knew them or not, and whether he'd given me warning or not. But I soon learned to enjoy the company, and realised that for many people, our home was a safe place.

My cousin Rod was a regular guest. The first time he visited it was harvest, and we spent a long time in the paddock helping the men with the bag sewing of the crop. I think Rod enjoyed being with us so much because he'd always wanted to be on the land. Visiting us gave him a taste of it. Rod brought his girlfriend Joy with him as their romance grew, and eventually they were married.

It was Rod who got me into being more adventurous with trying new foods. We have two big concrete silos on the farm, left over from the days when the farm had been a government training farm for returned soldiers. They stand in the paddock like two sentinels, but are never used. Rod was poking around in them and came back to the house with some dead pigeons.

"These would be nice for tea," he said.

I was not impressed but he was a guest, so I thought I had to do them. That posed a question—how do you cook pigeons? I knew I had to pluck them, clean them and then put them on to roast, but not really how to do that. I was still cooking with a wood stove at the time, so I decided to roast them in the same way I'd do any other roast. Rod, on the other hand, was right up with it, and between us I managed to serve a lovely meal of pigeon. I think this probably set me on the track to giving every new taste, a go.

Rod came in handy for quite a few other things over the years. Jim and I hadn't started with much, but as the family grew, so too did the items we collected. But where to fit them all? The cupboards were always overflowing. We had the sink cupboard under the window, and the multi-coloured cupboard along the side wall, but I still needed more space. As Rod was a cabinet maker, we employed him to build us cupboards along one wall in the kitchen. These cupboards were about six foot high and went from the door right to the office wall. On the door end there were another two smaller cupboards which housed the medicine cabinet. These sat on top of the fridge. I kept the top of that long bank of cupboards full of preserves I made each fruit season. These jars of preserved fruit fed the family each year. The first row was pride of place, and were always the cherries. I always opened the first bottle of cherries on Christmas day. Then there were peaches, nectarines, apricots, and pears, and finally the savoury jars like spaghetti and tomato juice.

So when we decided to move the kitchen into the small room on the north of the house, I called Rod to do the job. We decided to knock the wall out between the two rooms, making a walkway from the kitchen to the family room. I wanted a big pantry cupboard, but I told Rod I wanted the top of the cupboard to slope, so the men couldn't put anything on top of it. There's nothing so frustrating as when people leave things on the tops of cupboards.

"Well," Rod said, "I've never heard of that, but you can have a sloping top if you want." So he built it just the way I asked. When finished, I pointed it out to the men and said, "now you can't put anything up there." With that, Andrew removed his hat, and with a flick, tossed it up on top of the cupboard. I couldn't believe my eyes when it stayed there.

We have had so many other visitors over the years. We often had guest speakers from the church stay at our house for the night. Jim and I got to know many of them very well. Then there have been people who have been invited just because they were in town. Jim had a terrible habit of meeting someone new at the store or in the street, finding out where they were from, asking about their life, and before you knew it, inviting them home for a meal.

On another occasion, Jim was at the roadhouse in town when a young girl came in. She was riding a bike. While waiting to be served Jim did his usual twenty questions and found she was riding around the world. She'd come from

England and was on her way across Australia. Of course, he invited her home and she stayed for a few days.

In the 1960s Jim had the role of superintendent for the Methodist Sunday School. One day he was teaching his class outside when a group of young people came by looking for a church. When they saw Jim, they asked if they could join in his lesson. He soon realized they knew a lot more about the Bible than he did, but after the lesson he invited them home for lunch. I had already prepared just enough lunch for our family, but somehow, I had to come up with food for an extra five. I don't know how I managed it, but I did. But the result of this meeting was the beginning of a very active youth group, made up of overseas students. The leader of that group is still a close friend today.

It wasn't just Jim who would invite people around. Once our daughter Stephanie, who was in high school at the time, went to a dance at the hall, and the next thing we knew she was waking us up in the middle of the night. She'd brought home a couple of young men who'd come from afar on their motorbikes, thinking there would be rooms they could book for the night. But when they got to Melrose, they found there was no accommodation, so Stephanie invited them home to stay with us. We had no idea who they were or where they came from, but we made sure they had a place to stay.

During the 1970s and early 80s we had many people from youth group and church who would come to our house every Sunday night for tea. It became tradition to gather at the Bishops' for tea. It wasn't fancy, but it was memorable. Fried fishfingers and chips, followed by fruit salad and ice-cream for dessert. During that period of time, there were many people who came from other parts of Australia and overseas to study at Light Educational Ministries and most of them ended up at our house for tea some time or another. We had up to twenty or more people on some occasions. Even though I started out very shy, our home ended up being quite the community hub, and I enjoyed it. Everyone was welcome in our house.

24

SO, THIS IS CHRISTMAS

As one gets older, one can't help but reflect on how things have changed over the decades. Christmas is one of those times that always brings the memories back.

My memories of Christmas have always been special, even from when I was a child.

While World War Two was in progress, it didn't seem there was much of a fuss made over Christmas. How could there be, with so much strife in the world and so many of our loved ones fighting overseas? There were some events that still took place. Mum always took us to the John Martin's Christmas Pageant, which was started in 1933 by Sir Edward Hayward. This was always followed by a trip to the magic cave to see Father Christmas. We left our order for Christmas, got our stocking, and had a ride on Nimble and Nipper, the two huge rocking horses. But during the height of the war, the parade was cancelled.

Still, Mum always made sure there was a special present brought by Father Christmas. At times I worried he wouldn't make it. There was no such thing as air-conditioning in those days, and it was always so hot, so I'd toss and turn trying to get to sleep so Father Christmas would come.

I was in Grade 2, and Dad was home from war, when I had the first inkling that Father Christmas wasn't quite what he was supposed to be. I'd gone to bed early so I'd be well asleep and allow him to arrive, but it was just so hot, and I was having trouble getting to sleep. I was lying in my bed quietly when suddenly the door came open, and I could see Dad in the lounge room, setting up dolls house furniture on a big blanket box. Then he quietly went out and shut the door

The next morning I was thrilled with my gifts, but I wanted to know what Dad was doing, putting the Christmas presents out.

He was very quick about it.

"Father Christmas was running late, so I offered to help set the presents up for you," he told me. And apparently Father Christmas was very grateful for the help.

It didn't quite make me an unbeliever, but it started the process.

The first time I remember our family doing anything special for Christmas, was about 1948 or 1949. Don was home from the Navy and he'd brought some 78speed records which were played on a borrowed gramophone. Mum had gone to a lot of trouble to decorate, and Dad had brought in a big pine tree branch to set up as a tree in the lounge. It was covered with coloured streamers which Mum had made out of crepe paper. I thought it was the most beautiful thing I'd ever seen, and spent a lot of time playing around the tree. Don's records were stacked on the arm of a lounge chair next to the tree, and the gramophone sat on the other side. Although Margaret was eight years older than me, we still fought the way siblings do, and on this occasion we were having a ding-dong fight by the Christmas tree. I can't remember why, but during the fight Margaret pushed me, and I fell backwards, luckily onto the chair, unluckily right onto the stack of records, which were cleanly snapped in halves. The uproar that followed upset Christmas a bit.

But all too soon, I was married and had a family of my own, and it was time for me to make my own Christmas traditions.

After our marriage, things of faith began to become very clear to me. In our Christian community there was always a certain amount of argument about the right or wrong of having Father Christmas. Some would say, "it's all in fun so let the children have it," while others insisted "you are lying to the children so it is a sin." We had to make a decision about what we would do as the children came along. We decided that the truth should be told, so we brought the children up understanding the story of St Nicholas and explained that there was someone in each home who played the part of Father Christmas, but the secret was that none of the children knew who it was. We kept that up for quite a while, and as each child reached the age of ten, I took them aside and explained that this year they had been selected to be Father Christmas. They were to go to bed, and then when the others were asleep, I would come and get them to put the gifts under the tree and have the biscuits and milk left out for Father Christmas. We continued that until our youngest, Andrew, had his turn.

Christmas in Melrose was a grand affair. On Christmas Eve we always attended a service at the Methodist Church. When it was finished, a truck was brought up to the Church and my mother-in-law, Ella's, organ was placed on the back, right up by the cabin. Everyone climbed aboard, found a seat and away we would go, all around the town singing

Christmas carols on top note. When we came to houses where there were elderly people or where the family were very poor, we'd stop so one of the children could jump off the truck and take them a food parcel and Christmas cake made by the Ladies Fellowship.

That went on for many years, but eventually things changed and we began holding a Christmas in the Park event, alongside the Hall. Everyone would arrive around 6pm, bringing food for a pooled tea, and we'd sit around and chat while Christmas Carols were sung in the background. Afterwards, we'd all gather around while one of the ministers gave a Christmas message. After the message the children were told to be on the lookout for Father Christmas who was scheduled to come and give lollies and small gifts. The fun was that no one knew how he would come. On one occasion he arrived on the Fire truck, on another he turned up in a horse and jinker. Then on one occasion he left his costume behind and had to go back for it–he was very late arriving that year. I was the one who had to keep the children together while we waited and believe me, I had to do some quick thinking to keep them interested while the time ticked on.

Over the years, Christmas morning with five children developed into a definite routine. Everyone knew the rules— no one was allowed in the lounge until everyone was up, having made their bed and tidied their room. Then when we were all together, we'd gather around the tree, and Jim would read the scripture and give a short talk. Only then came the giving out of gifts, with paper going everywhere.

Our traditional breakfast was jellied cherries and ice cream. That might seem like an odd breakfast, but it started because I always bought a half-case of cherries to be preserved, and the first bottle was opened on Christmas Day.

It was always a loud and busy day—grandparents arrived mid-morning, with more gift giving, and then a hot roast lunch. After midday, the adults wanted to relax, so I kept a special pile of comics I'd buy over the year which were only read on Christmas Day while the adults rested. Once the energy was high again, the children would have a small concert to perform for the grandparents, which finished with a visit from a very little Father Christmas. By then, it was nearly time for bed.

As the children grew up, left home and started families of their own, the traditions were harder to keep. We started dividing Christmases, one year with our family at the farm house and the next with the spouses' families in the city. In our off years, Jim and I would go along with one of our children and spend Christmas with them and their other family. But now, our grandchildren have grown and started their own families, and there are even more in-laws to divide the time with. As we've gotten older, we've found the traditional large Christmas gatherings harder to host.

In 2021, we decided to do something different. Jim and I decided to remain at home. One day, we had some visitors around, and I asked what everyone was doing for Christmas. Our good friend Lyall popped up and said, "I don't know what I'm going to be doing; I have to talk to my son about it, he doesn't think he'll be able to get home, so that leaves me on my own."

"Well, that's no good. We'll have to get together." I threw the words into the conversation casually without giving it any serious thought.

Yvonne and Don were visiting at the same time, and Yvonne said she and Don would more than likely have Christmas on their own.

A couple of days later I received a phone call from Lyall.

"I'd like to accept your invitation to have Christmas with you."

I was flabbergasted. "I didn't really offer an invitation," I said, "but alright, that will be okay."

I called Yvonne and Don to see if they'd like to come too. In for a penny, in for a pound, as they say.

But I'm not as young as I used to be. And for years I've lost a lot of mobility, and can only move around using a walker. I cannot stand for more than about five minutes, and both Jim and I need at home support just to attend our daily tasks. So how was I going to get ready for Christmas day if I had visitors?

Bless my daughters. They got together and organised everything for me. I decided we'd have a cold collation for lunch. Prawn cocktail, cold meat and salads, and then pudding and custards. I also decided to be ambitious, and host our small gathering in our lounge room. This was a rare occasion—we mostly entertained at the kitchen table, so most of our visitors hadn't even seen the lounge. The girls were excited with a vision of how to transform the room— the place that was the centre of so much Christmas joy when they were young—into a special location for a shared lunch with friends. Together, we could get this done.

The first thing I needed to do was get the prawns from Caputos. I thought I'd have a trial run first, so when we were over at Port Pirie, I sat outside the place and gave Lyall and Jim very detailed instructions about buying the prawns. When I got them home I found they had got it wrong. Not to be beaten, I waited until we went to Pirie again, and this time I had it all written down. They must be prawns from local waters, all shelled, cleaned, cooked and prepared to eat. It worked perfectly. When we got home I took the prawns out of the bag and counted them to make sure I had enough for five people, and the few that were left over I made a little dressing for myself. They were absolutely beautiful. So they were stored away for Christmas.

Shortly after, Meredith rang and told me she would be here a couple of days before Christmas to stay overnight and help me set up everything ready for Christmas day. I only had the last things to see to on the morning. That was so kind, and a great relief for me, but I was still very concerned about the food. I decided that I would roast a chicken, get a ham and make four salads. In recent times I dislike making salads or food of any kind, so this was going to be quite a job. Luckily, when I was talking to Yvonne, she asked what she could bring along, offering two salads she had to make anyway. I'd decided to make the salad that Stephanie often makes from Chinese cabbage and when I mentioned this to Yvonne, she said she would do a tossed salad as well, so that took care of that.

While chatting to another friend, she commented that she'd bought her roast already: it was called the Ultimate Roast, chicken and duck stuffed into a turkey, with cranberry stuffing. That sounded good, so I asked her if she could get one for me when she was in Pt Augusta. When Lyall heard about this he said he would pay for it. My girls were still offering support—Meredith would make the pudding as always and also the mince pies, which get better every year; Stephanie bought the ham for us and several other bits and pieces for the salad; and Lee-Ann and Meredith came up and decorated the house. It was all coming together nicely.

Then we had the first problem. I was telling Yvonne what I had planned, and when I came to the meat, she said she thought some steak would be alright, instead of the roast beef.

"But I'm not doing beef," I said.

Then I found out Don didn't eat any poultry or mutton. In talking it through I found he loved prawns and is okay with ham, so we thought we could work it out—I could always not have the prawns and give Don the extra.

That evening I suggested we make our traditional cherries in jelly, because that could be made well before the day. Jim got to work to make them. To make jelly you put one cup of boiling water in the dish with the jelly crystals and dissolve them, then add a cup of cold water and fruit. I suggested to Jim that instead of adding a cup of cold water he should use the juice of the cherries, which he did. The next day I was sitting in front of the open fridge door and I noticed a jar on the top shelf, full of what looked like swollen blueberries. When I investigated, I found they were the smallest cherries I had ever seen, and there was no juice in the jar. It took me a little time to work it out, but eventually I called Jim and asked if he put the juice in the jelly.

"Yes. I did."

"Why didn't you put the cherries in the jelly as well?" I asked.

"You told me not to," he said.

I had to do some fast thinking, but I found there was plenty of room left in the dish, so I got him to make another jelly and this time put the cherries in as well.

From then, it all went as planned, Meredith and Lee-Ann arrived. They began getting things together immediately, stacking the crockery and cutlery on the traymobile and putting away things that didn't need to be out. Then they planned the next day, the 23rd – it was to be all hands on deck, decorating and setting up so everything was done except that which must be left until the last minute.

The morning dawned and we got up bright and early. We had just sat down to breakfast when Meredith appeared at the door and announced, "I'm not well." On investigation it was decided she had an infection which needed medical help. She had rung the doctor in Adelaide during the night, and been told they'd would arrange for her to get some medication from the local pharmacy as soon as it was open. I was well aware of this disease that had come upon her so I insisted she rest. However, it wasn't long and Andrew and family arrived, out of the blue, to say they "just wanted to pick up a few things and say Merry Christmas to us." This was a good thing, as my daughter-in-law Tonya could see I was stressed and was able to give a hand with one or two things. I began to get worried as I could see I couldn't do the job anymore.

At some time during all of this, Lyall came in for a cuppa, which was lucky as during the conversation he told me he didn't eat prawns.

"Oh no," I thought, and then, "wait this is good." I could give Don more prawns. But hang on, what would I do about Lyall while we had our prawn cocktail?

I had the idea of putting a small cheese platter on the table which he could use, and others could have some as well if they wanted. That would be so easy, so I casually asked Lyall if he liked cheese.

"No," was Lyall's reply. "I've never liked it much."

Well that was it, I'd make a dip and that would be what he would have.

We got Meredith and Lee-Ann on their way home to the city as soon as we could. Meredith kept saying "What else has to be done?" Of course there was a great deal still to be done, but I was more concerned about getting her home and resting. Once they were on the road, I set about making lists of everything I had to get done so that it would all go smoothly the next day.

Stephanie had given me strict instructions about making the salad and she'd supplied all the ingredients, so I just had to put it all together the next day. She also had given us a half leg of ham which I thought would be easy to slice up.

Christmas Eve arrived. I had to make up the salad I was providing to the point of putting the dressing on which would be done the next day. I had to roast the Ultimate Roast, carve the ham, and place everything on a nice platter ready for tomorrow. I had to make a dip, ready for Lyall's entrée. And I had to make the sauce for the prawns. And finally, I wanted to get the table all set and ready for the morning. I told Jim I needed him to be here all the time as I had so much to do; I had to rely on him to help me do the things I couldn't. So, I wasn't too pleased when I heard him inviting a friend in for a cuppa in the morning. Not long after that Jim announced that he was going to Booleroo because he had left his glasses at the church. I tried to make him understand I needed him here, but he felt his glasses were more important. I stayed and did what I could, but there was little I could manage without someone to help me with lifting and leg work. I waited and waited thinking he'd be back quite quickly, but no. What other things he did I don't know, but it sure took a long time—he wasn't back until past lunch time. Then, as soon as we had lunch, he said he had to go out and fix a water leak. Now I know things like water leaks have to be seen to, but so far I'd had no help at all for the day and still a lot to go. I had to get inventive. I used my wheels to transport small things from the kitchen to the lounge room, and for the larger items I used the traymobile; I put things onto it and then lay on it for support pushing it to wherever I needed it. Finally, when the later part of the day came, Jim was ready to help. I admit I was furious, to say nothing of being exceptionally tired, but together we managed to get some of it finished, though there was still a lot to do on Christmas morning.

And then the day arrived. We got up as we usually would, hurriedly gave each other our presents, and Jim rushed down to the kitchen to get on with breakfast. Out came the jelly, cream and ice-cream—the tradition we have never given up—and then it was time to be getting things ready for lunch. The sauce was added to the prawns, and dip and biscuits put on the table. The meat had to be cut up and I had it planned in my head how to make it really pretty. I took the roast out of the fridge prepared to slice it in nice thin slices, but the moment it was cut it all fell to pieces, and I was left to serve it in great lumps. Then I tried the ham, but I did no better. I couldn't get a full slice because of the bones. So my fancy serving disappeared, but when I taste tested, the meat was delicious. Finally, we were ready. We put out drinks in the lounge plus some nibblies and mince pies, and then sat down and waited for the guests to come.

I had told them to arrive around 11am, I put on some carols, but only softly for mood music, and we waited, and we waited, and we waited. By 11.30am I commented that I was surprised that Lyall wasn't there as he is usually very punctual. But we kept waiting, and waiting, and waiting, and even began to nod off a bit. At 11.45am I said to Jim, "You best give Lyall a ring and see what's happening."

And so he did.

Ring, ring.

"Hello," said Lyall.

"Hello," said Jim. "Where are you?"

"Here."

"What do you mean, *here*?"

"We're here sitting in your kitchen!"

With a start, we headed out to the kitchen, where we

found our guests had settled themselves in, just sitting there, chatting. We couldn't believe it. They hadn't questioned their lack of hosts, or even a lack of Christmas setup. But we soon had them in the lounge, glass in hand, and all enjoying our Christmas together.

It was a far cry from my childhood days during war time when having a refrigerator was a luxury—the world looked completely different now. It was also a much quieter affair than when our home was full of small children, each taking turns to play Father Christmas.

But we sat together, five 'oldies' in the 21st century sharing memories and plenty of laughter, it was just as special.

25

A NEW STAGE OF LIFE

Many years ago I became quite sick with what seemed to be a mystery disease. It started off as a very bad cold, but instead of slowly getting better, it seemed to just hang on. There were quite a few people with it in our district, and the doctor commented to me that a lot of the women who had these symptoms were wives of Hospital Board members.

He kept taking blood and sending it away to pathology, always getting the same result—until one day they actually rang him from pathology and asked what was going on, as they were getting repeated blood tests that showed nothing. When he was talking to them it suddenly clicked and they tested for Ross River fever. They found the culprit, more than likely a mosquito. That fixed things up and I was soon recovering, but I was warned that I might get rheumatoid arthritis. I hoped desperately that I wouldn't, but to no avail. I developed it, and I had to adjust.

Very slowly things began to change. It seemed to be getting harder to do what I had found easy in the past, but I put it down to age. After all, you can't expect to stay young forever. Then one day I was just washing my hands in the bathroom when I noticed everything looked strange, as in, I could only see a half of everything. *That's odd*, I thought. I decided to go to the family room and sit down. I got to the table and went to move something on it and found I couldn't move the object or my hand. Things were getting worse.

Then, thankfully, there was a knock at the door and a man came in who I didn't know. He said he had borrowed our ute and was just returning the keys, but I couldn't communicate with him. I managed to indicate that I was in trouble, and got him to get Jim. Suddenly there seemed to be people everywhere and I was quickly taken to the hospital. When I arrived, I still couldn't speak or communicate. People were moving around at speed and the next thing I knew, I was being prepared to go with the flying doctor. They flew me to Adelaide with a stroke, and there I was nursed back to health. But even though I recovered, my life was changed. It didn't change in a hurry but it has changed slowly. All day I feel as if I have some pain somewhere, and there is nothing I can do about it. When I came out of the hospital, Stephanie saw a small set of wheels in the second-hand shop next to her salon and she bought them for me. Thankfully they have seen me through, because if I hadn't had them I would not have been able to move around. All this time Jim has been my offsider, and we have operated by me giving instructions and he following. But as with all things, we are wearing out, and Jim has found it hard to do the necessary things around the place. Eventually we reached the point that we had to accept it was time to leave our beautiful home and go to the Mt View Homes to live.

It is quite pleasant here, and we are well looked after, but it's not home. But we will make the best of it as our good Lord has supplied, and He knows His plan for us.

EDITORS NOTE: Jennette wrote this last section in December 2023, well before she had finished writing everything she wanted to. She must have realised she needed an ending, 'just in case'.

Three months later, on February 29th, 2024, she took a turn which the doctors at the Port Pirie Hospital said she would not recover from. Her whole family, including Tim who took an urgent flight from Sydney, were with her when she passed from this life into the arms of her eternal Saviour, March 1st, 2024 at 4am. She was eighty-five years old.

RECIPES FOR CHRISTMAS

CHERRIES AND JELLY

Ingredients:
　　Canned cherries
　　Port Wine Jelly

Make up the Jelly according to the pack instructions, only replace half the water with Cherry syrup. Add the cherries to the jelly before refrigerating to set. Serve with Ice-cream on Christmas morning.

PRAWN COCKTAIL DRESSING

Ingredients:
　　300 ml cream
　　Tomato sauce (ketchup)
　　Worcestershire sauce (Holbrooks is best)
　　Salt to taste

Method:

Whip Cream until stiff. Add several dashes of tomato sauce and Worcestershire sauce until the colour is dusty pink. Add a pinch of salt.

Taste. Add more sauce and salt to taste. It should not taste like cream, but have a good savoury bite.

GREAT GRAN'S CHRISTMAS PUDDING

This recipe was given to Jennette in 1965 when Great Gran (Emily Elizabeth Thistleton) was 86 years old. She never had the recipe written down and so when Jennette asked if she could have it, Emily invited her into her house to show her how to make her puddings. Jennette converted what she observed to metric. If you can use the old measurements, it might be better.

Jennette passed this recipe to me (Meredith Resce) in the 1990s. Over the years I have made it every Christmas, and have adjusted according to the times we live in. Remember, Emily made this pudding in the late 1800s-early 1900s without the benefit of electricity and other fangled developments.

INGREDIENTS

½ lb. (225 gm) butter
1 cup milk
1 ½ cups sugar
4 eggs
1 teaspoon ground ginger
2 teaspoons nutmeg
2 teaspoons mixed spices

3 cups S.R. Flour
pinch salt
2 teaspoons bicarbonate of soda
3 cups plain flour
1lb. (450gm) currants
1 lb (450 gm) sultanas
½ lb (225 gm) dates
2 tablespoons mixed peel
1 lb (450 gm) chopped raisins
1 tablespoon plum jam
2 tablespoons brandy

METHOD

Mix together flour and fruit, spice, salt, nutmeg and ginger.

In another bowl cream butter and sugar

Add eggs one at a time, and mix well

Add milk with carb soda dissolved in it, to the brandy and jam.

Combine two mixtures well.

Wet pudding cloth in hot water and sprinkle well with flour.

Place pudding in cloth and tie a little above the mixture to allow for expansion.

Place in boiling water keeping the top of the cloth held up by the lid of the pot to stop the water getting into the pudding.

Steam for 4 hours. (2 or 3 hours when you make it and then the remainder of the time on Christmas Day)

Keep adding a little water so that the level doesn't get to far down.

This should be made at the end of November or early

December, then hung until Christmas Day. This makes one huge pudding or two very big puddings.

You can make one big one for Christmas Day and two small ones to use over the holidays.

In these modern times, I have used a chicken or turkey-sized oven bag instead of the pudding cloth. This means none of the pudding is wasted (there is always a certain amount that makes a shell that is not nice to eat when a cloth is used) and there isn't the messy washing of the cloth after.

However, if you use the oven bags instead, preparation is slightly different. Recently, I make the puddings mid-December and freeze them (this avoids the small chance of the pudding going moldy). I pull the pudding out on the day it is to be used, and it thaws. When it is pudding time, I ask who wants a piece (not everyone likes pudding – don't ask me why). I cut the required number of slices and put in a microwave oven proof dish, sprinkle each piece with a couple teaspoons of water. This is to make up for the moisture that is lost in not doing the extra boiling. Then pop into the microwave for 30-60 seconds, or until hot.

Serve with loads of custard (if you're in the northern hemisphere for a cold Christmas) or ice-cream (if you're in the southern hemisphere for a warm Christmas)

www.ingramcontent.com/pod-product-compliance
Lightning Source LLC
Chambersburg PA
CBHW071956290426
44109CB00018B/2045